THE COMEDY OF MANNERS

English Literature

Editor
PROFESSOR JOHN LAWLOR
MA(OXON), FSA
Professor of English Language and Literature
in the University of Keele

THE COMEDY OF
MANNERS

Kenneth Muir
King Alfred Professor of English Literature
in the University of Liverpool

HUTCHINSON UNIVERSITY LIBRARY
LONDON

HUTCHINSON & CO (*Publishers*) LTD
178–202 Great Portland Street, London W1

London Melbourne Sydney
Auckland Bombay Toronto
Johannesburg New York

First published 1970

The illustration to The Way of The World *on
the cover of the paperback edition was taken
from an engraving in Congreve's Collected
Works, by courtesy of the Victoria and Albert
Museum*

*This book has been set in Times, printed in Great Britain
on Smooth Wove paper by Anchor Press, and
bound by Wm. Brendon, both of Tiptree, Essex*

09 100481 0   (paper)
09 100480 2   (cased)

CONTENTS

PREFACE

This book owes most to the genius of Dame Edith Evans whose Millamant and Mrs Sullen were a revelation to my generation of the theatrical effectiveness of the Comedy of Manners. It also owes a great deal to the published work and conversation of Professor Bonamy Dobrée; to amateur actors at Leeds and elsewhere with whom I have been associated; and to Mrs Inga-Stina Ewbank and Dr Norman Sherry for reading the book in manuscript.

Thanks are due to Professors John Russell Brown and Bernard Harris and to the publishers of Stratford-upon-Avon Studies, Edward Arnold, for permitting me to include some sections of an essay I contributed to *Restoration Theatre* and to them and Mrs Anne Barton for allowing me to quote from her essay on Wycherley.

The book incorporates the substance of the first H. O. White Memorial Lecture which I had the honour of delivering at Trinity College, Dublin, in April 1969.

Liverpool   KENNETH MUIR

I

INTRODUCTION

This book is concerned with Restoration comedy and with those plays written in the eighteenth century which were an attempt to capture something of its spirit. The plays are usually entitled 'comedy of manners' or 'artificial comedy'. Neither title is satisfactory; for 'artificial' implies that the plays are divorced from real life and 'manners' suggests that they deal only with superficial characteristics of men and women, imposed by a sophisticated and artificial society rather than with the permanent manifestations of human nature and with universal human problems.

If one examines comedies of different ages—*Lysistrata, Twelfth Night, Volpone, Troilus and Cressida, Man and Superman, The Playboy of the Western World,* and *Le Misanthrope*—of which only one could be classified as a comedy of manners, it is nevertheless obvious that each one is coloured by the manners of the age in which they were written. Jack Tanner is unthinkable in Illyria or the Playboy in Athens. Lysistrata would not be at home in Célimène's Parisian drawing-room; and although Troilus and Alceste are both serious-minded men who fall in love with flirts, Alceste's predicament is partly determined by the society in which he lives.

On the other hand, if one considers plays which all critics would classify as comedies of manners—*The Country Wife, The Way of the World, The School for Scandal*—it is equally obvious that the authors of these plays were concerned with fundamental questions of human behaviour—in fact, with morals—as well as with the superficial and transient manners of an age.[1]

[1] Mr Norman N. Holland is right when he says (in *The First Modern Comedies,* p. 4) that the comedies of the period are concerned with the conflict between 'manners' (i.e. social conventions) and anti-social, 'natural', desires.

The critics are doubtless right to regard the English comedies written during the half-century following the Restoration as belonging to a special *genre*, and differing from those written before the closing of the theatres, as well as from the sentimental comedies of the eighteenth century. Yet there are two good reasons why we should not try to make an absolute segregation. First, because, as we shall see, there are many links between the comedies written before 1640 and those written after 1660. The second reason is, from the theatrical point of view, more important. To regard the plays as 'artificial' has an unfortunate influence on the way they are performed. Nigel Playfair deserves our gratitude for showing that Restoration comedies could still delight modern audiences and for enabling playgoers to see Edith Evans as Millamant, Mrs Fondlewife and Mrs Sullen; but in those productions at the Lyric Theatre, Hammersmith, delightful as they were, too much stress was laid on externals —fans, lace handkerchiefs, snuff-boxes, muffs, frills, etc.—and the behaviour which goes with them, and too little on the essential passions of the heart. Playfair may be forgiven because, as a pioneer, he was uncertain of the reception the plays were likely to receive after they had been banished from the stage for over a century. More recent producers have less excuse.

It is necessary to emphasise the basic differences between the Elizabethan and Restoration theatre. In 1610 there were at least six theatres open in London; in the Restoration period there were never more than two, and sometimes there was only one, despite the enormous increase of population during the intervening sixty years. In the Commonwealth period, when the theatres were closed, people had got out of the habit of playgoing; and, presumably, a section of the population had been influenced by Puritan propaganda against the stage. The audiences were drawn mainly from the upper classes and their hangers-on and the plays naturally reflected their tastes and attitudes.

The physical characteristics of the theatre had likewise changed. The apron and the balcony above the stage had gone; the theatre was no longer open to the sky but lit by artificial light; there were no groundlings, but seats for all; no one could sit on the stage, as in Shakespeare's day; and the main stage was retracted behind a proscenium arch and provided with a front curtain. In place of an unlocalised scene and a bare stage, the new theatres made use of painted sets.

Another important difference was that after the re-opening of the theatres female rôles were taken, as in France, by actresses. This fact had a considerable influence on the treatment of sexual relations, especially, perhaps, as many of the actresses were not reputed to be models of chastity.

The stage always reflects the society for which it caters; and playgoers in the reign of Charles II followed the king himself in seizing on a sexual freedom which would have been unthinkable during the interregnum, and, despite the tone of some of the cavalier poets, not generally acceptable in the reign of Charles I. This licentiousness was bound to be reflected in the comedies of the period. It has also been argued that the courtiers brought back from their exile a taste for French drama. It is certainly true that English heroic tragedy owes a great deal to French classical tragedy and Dryden's prefaces owed a debt to the *examens* with which Corneille prefaced his plays. But the influence of French comedy— at least in the years immediately following the Restoration—has probably been exaggerated. It must be remembered that Molière's first great play was not performed till 1662. Later on there were specific debts to *L'Ecole des Femmes, Le Misanthrope, Tartuffe* and to several other plays. But by this time the main lines of development for English comedy were already laid down.

Restoration comedy is nearly all concerned with Londoners of a single class. Exceptions such as *Bury Fair, The Recruiting Officer* and *The Beaux' Stratagem* will be discussed in later chapters; but in most of these there is a contrast between metropolitan and provincial manners, and even where the setting is nominally in Italy or Sicily the gallants are obviously, if not purely, English. In contrast to this, none of Shakespeare's comedies has a London setting and only one, *The Merry Wives of Windsor*, has avowedly English characters. Other Elizabethan plays are set in London, but these are concerned with rogues (as in *The Alchemist*) or citizens, and not with society. Nevertheless the satirical portraits of the citizens and the way in which they are frequently outwitted finds a counterpart in many Restoration comedies. The cuckolds, such as Fondlewife, belong to the citizen class; and there are some plays of the period which are not very different in spirit from Jacobean citizen comedy, although they are generally less moral in their conclusions. This can be shown by a consideration of *The London Cuckolds* (1681). The author, Edward Ravenscroft was not a particularly original, and certainly not a brilliant, dramatist; and, for that reason, the play is useful for purposes of comparison. It depends more on its bustling action than on its dialogue. Three London merchants try to avoid their marital destiny by different means. Dashwell thinks his wife Eugenia

is virtuous merely because she pretends to be; but she cuckolds him
when the one man she has really loved returns from abroad in
disguise. Alderman Wiseacres follows the plan adopted by Pinchwife
in Wycherley's play of marrying an innocent country girl; but, as
comic retribution demands, Peggy's ignorance ensures her fall. She
is seduced by the sexually unsuccessful Ramble, after he has failed
to win the other two wives, and in the attempt has got caught in a
cellar window, been set on fire by a link—a fire which is extinguished
by the contents of a chamber-pot—had his face blacked, and been
arrested.

Alderman Doodle, whose wife Arabella is a pretender to wit,
thinks to safeguard her chastity by making her promise to say No.
Although she keeps her word, she is the first of the three wives to
be seduced. Her seducer is Townley, who is described as 'careless
of Women, but fortunate'. Like several Restoration gallants, he is
bored by the ease of his conquests and does his best to help his
friend Ramble. This is part of the scene with Arabella.

Town. Madam, I am your most humble Servant.
Arab. No.
Town. Y'Gad but I am, and will if you please.
Arab. No.
Town. Will you not give me leave to wait on you?
Arab. No.
Town. Nor stand and talk with you a little, dear Rogue?
Arab. No.
Town. I am in love with you; will you be hard-hearted to a man that
    loves you?
Arab. No.
Town. By Jove I would kiss thee for that, but that I fear 'twould put you
    out of humour.
Arab. No. [*Townley kisses her.*]
Town. That was kindly said—there—Now shall I wait on you to your
    door?
Arab. No . . .
Town. Must I then be gone and leave you?
Arab. No.
Town. By her answering *No* to contraries, I find she has taken a humour
    to say nothing else, I will fit her with Questions; now Lady answer
    me at your Peril. Beware you don't tell me a lye: Are you a
    Maid?
Arab. Ha, ha, ha!
Town. . . . Is your Husband at home?
Arab. No.

Town. Would you refuse a Bed-fellow in his room tonight if you lik'd
    the Man?
Arab. No.
Town. If I go home with you, will you thrust me out?
Arab. No.
Town. Nor if I come to Bed to you?
Arab. No, no, no, no, no.—Ha, ha, ha.

More significant than the survival of some attitudes of citizen
comedy is the fact that Ben Jonson's method was admired and
imitated by Restoration dramatists. This is apparent from the
frequent references to Jonson in the criticism of the period—in
Dryden's *Essay of Dramatic Poesy*, for example, in Shadwell's
prefaces, and in Congreve's discussion of humour in comedy—from
the influence of the theory of humours on many of the dramatists,
and in the naming of characters—Mrs Loveit, Lady Wishfort,
Witwoud, Petulant, Fainall—and above all in that Restoration
comedy, unlike the Romantic comedy of Shakespeare, was essentially
satirical.

Jonson's style, however, appeared to audiences and critics to be
more old-fashioned than that of Beaumont and Fletcher, whose
plays were popular after the Restoration. The conversation and the
behaviour of their heroes seemed to be closer than either Jonson's
or Shakespeare's to that of the gentlemen of the new age—and,
therefore, it may be said, less like real gentlemen; and the very
qualities which make modern critics adopt a dismissive attitude to
Beaumont and Fletcher would, if anything, have increased their
popularity. Farquhar's *The Inconstant* is an adaptation of Fletcher's
The Wild Goose Chase, of which the hero, like that of *The Way of the
World*, is called Mirabel. He keeps a book of his conquests, as Don
Giovanni was to do. Like any Restoration gallant he is violently
averse to marriage, although he is finally cornered. Mirabel and
Oriana are forerunners of what John H. Smith calls 'the gay couple'
who appear so frequently in Restoration comedy.

Other examples of 'the gay couple' are to be found in two of
Shirley's plays, *The Witty Fair One* (1628) and *Hyde Park* (1632);
and some critics have regarded these plays and *The Lady of Pleasure*
(1635) as comedies of manners. Shirley, declares Miss Lynch,
portrays polite society with approval.[1]

It is a society obviously more sophisticated than the fashionable world

[1] *The Social Mode of Restoration Comedy,* p. 37.

of Fletcher's plays. Manners have become crystallised into a formal system. With thorough self-consciousness Shirley's characters adopt a social pose. They play a social game in which every gesture is observed and every move counts.

These remarks seem to exaggerate the resemblances and ignore the differences between Shirley's plays and Restoration comedy; and it is doubtful whether his world is more sophisticated than Fletcher's. Aimwell, in *The Witty Fair One*, who marries Violetta despite her father's plans, is no different from dozens of successful lovers in Elizabethan plays; and the stratagem by which the father's choice, Sir Nicholas Treedle, is married to a chambermaid can be paralleled in earlier plays, even though the trick was used by Congreve and other Restoration dramatists. The other couple in the play, Fowler and Penelope, are in love with each other; but Fowler hopes to attain his ends without marriage. In the end Penelope makes him agree to marry her, first, by tricking him into breaking a vow, and then by pretending that he is a ghost, since he is 'dead to virtue'. Fowler agrees to reform:

> Witness my death to vanity, quitting all
> Unchaste desires:—revise me in thy thoughts,
> And I will love as thou hast taught me, nobly
> And like a husband, by this kiss, the seal
> That I do shake my wanton slumber off,
> And wake to virtue.

In *Hyde Park*, Julietta converts Lord Bonvile from illicit love to matrimony by delivering an excellent sermon on the incompatibility of nobility and lust. Obviously the moralising of Penelope and Julietta would have seemed out of place after the Restoration. But the courtship of Mistress Carol, a professed enemy to love, by Fairfield is much closer to the style of the comedy of manners. Fairfield eventually makes her fall in love with him by making her promise never to do so.

The Lady of Pleasure has a wife who lures her husband up to town and there cuckolds him; and her scorn of the country and its pleasures in the first scene was to be echoed by many Restoration wives. But there the resemblance ends. Lady Bornwell repents of her single act of adultery; and Sir Thomas cures her of her extravagance by pretending to be more extravagant himself. Celestina, a young widow, who also begins by being extravagant, ends by making Lord A ashamed of himself for having attempted to seduce her.

There is, in one of her speeches, a reference to the lesson of chastity set by Charles I and his queen; and we may suspect that Shirley in all these comedies adopted a moral tone partly to please the Court. But they seem to have more resemblance to sentimental comedy than to the comedy of manners.

There are several other dramatists who have been put forward as forerunners of Restoration comedy—D'Avenant, Cockain and Richard Brome. Perhaps, as Swinburne and Bonamy Dobrée suggested, Brome's *A Mad Couple Well Match'd* is nearest in spirit to later comedy of manners. The hero, Careless, who is rewarded with a wealthy widow at the end of the play, is as much a libertine as any Restoration gallant; and, although Brome was one of Jonson's followers, he seems not to disapprove of his hero's conduct.

No one play contains all the typical characteristics of post-Restoration comedy—libertinism, opposition between town and country and between gallant and citizen, male reluctance to marry, wives' dissatisfaction with husbands, witty repartee, and a realistic portrayal of manners—but it is nevertheless true that in the last ten years before the closing of the theatres English comedy was moving in the direction of the comedy of manners and providing a more realistic picture of society than it had done in the reigns of Elizabeth I and James I.

The term 'Restoration comedy' is loosely applied to the plays written between 1660 and 1710, a period of fifty years. A period of the same length covered the whole range of 'Elizabethan' drama from the work of the university wits to the closing of the theatres. The difference between Etherege and Farquhar is not as great as that between Lyly and Shirley, but it is nevertheless significant; and it is important to realise the differences not merely between one dramatist and another, but also between the societies for which they wrote. The plays covered four reigns—Charles II, James II, William and Mary, Anne—and the greatest dramatist, Congreve, was not born when Etherege's first plays were performed. At the end of the period, the climate of the age had completely changed. *The Tatler* began publication in 1709, and *The Spectator* two years later; and before the end of the seventeenth century sentimental comedy had begun to oust the comedy of manners. Addison has been described, with some justice, as a forerunner of the Victorians. This means that the dramatists at the end of the period were not attempting to write the same kind of play as those at the beginning. There had been a reaction against the indecency and immorality of the earlier comedies and for this there was some justification if only because there had been some improvement in the morals of society.

There had been sporadic attacks on the stage throughout the period. Many of them are quoted by Joseph Wood Krutch in *Comedy and Conscience after the Restoration*. John Evelyn, for example, who later approved of Wycherley's plays, wrote to a friend in 1664:

You know, my Lord, that I . . . am far from Puritanism; but I would have no reproach left our adversaries in a thing which may so conveniently be reform'd. Plays are now with us become a licentious excess, and a vice, and need severe censors that should look as well to their morality, as to their lines and numbers.

Baxter in 1673 complained that the plays of his age were 'not only sins, but heinous aggravated sins'. James Wright made one of his speakers in *Country Conversations* (1694)[1] declare

that the common parts and characters of our modern comedy are two young debauchés whom the author calls men of wit and pleasure, and sometimes men of wit and sense—The bottle and the Miss (as they phrase it) twisted together make their Summum Bonum; all their songs and discourse is on that subject. But at last, partly for variety of faces, and partly in consideration of improving their estate (shatter'd with keeping) they marry two young ladies, one of which is as wild as possibly can be, so as to 'scape the main chance, the other, more reserved, but really as forward to be marry'd as her sister.

Blackmore, in the preface to *Prince Arthur* (1695), made a similar protest,[1] and one of the dramatists, Thomas Shadwell, complained in *The Royal Shepherdess* (1669) that

It pleases most to see Vice incouraged, by bringing The Characters of debauch'd People upon the Stage, and making them pass for fine Gentlemen, who openly profess Swearing, Drinking, Whoring, breaking Windows, beating Constables, etc.[2]

[1] cf. Krutch, op. cit., pp. 93–4, 98–9.
[2] cf. It is a Vertuous Play, you will confess
Where Vicious men meet their deserv'd success.
Not like our Modern ones, where still we find
Poets are onely to the Ruffians kind;
And give them still the Ladies in the Play,
But 'faith their Ladies are as bad as they.

It will be seen from these quotations that not everyone approved of the moral tone of the comedy of the period; and Wright's summary of a typical plot is not much of a distortion. The dramatists could have pleaded in their defence that their plays were a true picture of society—or, at least, of one section of society. Their portraits of gallants were true to life, as 'The Character of a Town Gallant' (1678) illustrates:

> His Trade is making of *Love*, yet he knows no difference between that and *Lust*, and tell him of a *Virgin* at Sixteen, he shall swear then *Miracles* are not ceas'd. He is so bitter an Enemy to *Marriage*, that one would suspect him born out of *Lawfull Wedlock*. For he never hears Matrimony nam'd but he sweats and starts as bad as at the Salute of a *Sergeant* and has 40 lines of *Conjugium Conjurgium* got ready by heart to rail at it. But for the most delicious Recreation of *Whoring*, he protests a Gentleman cannot live without it.

The dramatists could claim that their portraits of gallants were in the spirit of this satirical sketch and that, in accordance with the Renaissance theory which goes back to Aristotle, they wrote their comedies to ridicule the vices and faults of the characters they depicted. But, as Dryden points out in his preface to *An Evening's Love* (1671):

> The business of the poet is to make you laugh: when he writes humour, he makes folly ridiculous; when wit, he moves you, if not always to laughter, yet to a pleasure that is more noble. And if he works a cure on folly, and the small imperfections in mankind, by exposing them to public view, that cure is not performed by an immediate operation. For it works first on the ill nature of the audience; they are moved to laugh by the representation of deformity; and the shame of that laughter teaches us to amend what is ridiculous in our manners.

Dryden goes on to claim that he does not write to make libertinism amiable. He and other dramatic poets

> make not vicious persons happy, but only as Heaven makes sinners so; that is, by reclaiming them first from vice. For so 'tis to be supposed they are, when they resolve to marry.

Most modern critics believe that Dryden and the other dramatists were self-deluded or disingenuous about their motives and that they did not really expect the audience to condemn the libertinism of their gallants. Here, as we shall see in later chapters, it is important to distinguish between Etherege and Wycherley, and between Congreve and Farquhar.

For many years the complaints about the moral tone of the comedies had no apparent effect; and the surprising success of Jeremy Collier's *Short View of the Immorality and Profaneness of the English Stage* (1698) was due more to a shift in public opinion than to any merits of this curious book. Literary critics, on the whole, have been singularly kind to Collier and most of them, led by Johnson and Macaulay, have assumed that he routed his opponents and that all the replies of the dramatists were feeble. Collier made a few valid criticisms, but the general tone of his book is intemperate and absurd. One can only assume that critics have praised Collier because they think Restoration comedy is immoral, and not for the strength of his arguments or for the beauty of his style. He seems incapable of distinguishing between a good argument and a completely irrelevant one. He does not distinguish between harmless oaths and real blasphemy, nor does he allow the stage to reflect the language of the age. He stigmatises Lady Froth's calling Jehu a hackney coachman as profane[1]—in fact he misinterprets the passage—and when Vainlove asks Belmour if he could be content to go to heaven and he replies, 'Hum, not immediately in my conscience, not heartily', Collier regards it as blasphemous.[2] He complains[3] that

Lord *Foplington* [*sic*] laughs at the publick Solemnities of Religion, as if 'twas a ridiculous piece of Ignorance, to pretend to the Worship of a God. He discourses with *Berinthia* and *Amanda* in this manner: *Why Faith Madam,—Sunday is a vile Day, I must confess. A man must have very little to do at Church that can give an account of the Sermon.*

What Collier fails to realise is that for a fool to dislike church-going is an oblique tribute to it.

Cynthia in *The Double Dealer* remarks: 'I am thinking that tho' Marriage makes Man and Wife one Flesh, it leaves them still two Fools'. Collier complains:[4] 'This Jest is made upon a Text in *Genesis*, and afterwards applyed by our Saviour to the Case of Divorse'. (Congreve showed that by leaving out a word Collier had altered the meaning.) These are typical examples of the profanity Collier professes to find in the comedies he examines and it is not surprising that the dramatists were nonplussed.

[1] op. cit., p. 64.
[2] ibid., p. 62.
[3] ibid., p. 78.
[4] ibid., p. 82.

Collier devotes one chapter to a matter on which he feels particularly keenly, that the dramatists satirise the clergy. This he regards as intolerable because of their relation to the Deity, because of the importance of their office, and because their function has been held in esteem 'in all ages, and countries'.[1] But, of course, a playwright has every right to satirise a hypocritical, time-serving or foolish clergyman.

There are two other matters on which Collier feels strongly: that the poets 'make *Women* speak smuttily'[2] and that the nobility are satirised. On the first point he argues that women without modesty are monsters, and that modesty is the distinguishing virtue of that sex. On the satirising of noble lords, he asks:[3]

Must all Men be handled alike? Must their Roughness be needs play'd upon Title? And can't they lash the Vice without pointing upon the *Quality*? . . . Why are not the Decencies of Life, and the Respects of Conversation observ'd? . . . What necessity is there to kick the *Coronets* about the *Stage*, and to make a Man a Lord, only in order to make him a coxcomb [?].

The answer to both complaints is that not all women are modest and not all lords are sensible: and those who are immodest or foolish are legitimate targets for the satirist.

In his final chapter Collier gives the opinion of the Church concerning the stage. Players, for example, were excommunicated in A.D. 314; Theophilus thought it sinful to attend plays; Tertullian condemned plays for their superstition and idolatry; St Chrisostome said that the playhouse 'has brought Whoring and Ribaldry into Vogue, and finish'd all the parts of Debauchery'. But the views of the Fathers on the Roman theatre cannot really be applied to the theatre in the seventeenth century; and the extreme puritanism of some of Collier's citations shows that the Fathers would have liked to ban all the arts. Lactantius says that

A well work'd *Poem* is a powerful piece of Imposture: It masters the Fancy, and hurries it no Body knows whither.—If therefore we would be govern'd by Reason, let us stand off from the Temptation, such Pleasures can have no good Meaning. Like delicious Morsels they subdue the Palate, and flatter us only to cut our Throats.

[1] ibid., p. 127.
[2] ibid., p. 8.
[3] ibid., pp. 175–6.

In the whole of Collier's treatise he makes only two valid points, and these are lost in a maze of irrelevancies. It is true that many of the plays contain bawdy and indecency[1] and some dramatists introduce them to amuse the audience as well as to reflect the colloquial speech of the time. Different ages have different standards in these matters and most people today are not offended by the bawdy. It is arguable that a dramatist who wishes to satirise the sexual behaviour of his age is bound to be indecent. The more moral he is, the more indecent he will be. One of the most indecent passages in the whole of Restoration comedy—the 'china scene' in Wycherley's *The Country Wife*—is extremely funny as well as outrageous. It exemplifies brilliantly the hypocrisy of Lady Fidget and Mrs Squeamish and is therefore moral in its effect.

The other valid point made by Collier is contained in the title of Chapter 4, 'The Stage-Poets make their Principal Persons Vitious, and reward them at the End of the Play'. It is true that some drama-tists—though not the better ones—depict witty rakes with sympathy and allow them to win the hand of the beautiful heiress in the last act of the play. There is some justification for Collier's outburst:[2]

Here you have a Man of Breeding and Figure that burlesques the *Bible*, Swears, and talks Smut to Ladies, speaks ill of his Friend behind his Back, and betraies his Interest. A fine Gentleman that has neither Honesty, nor Honour, Conscience, nor Manners, Good Nature, nor civil Hypocricy. Fine, only in the Insignificancy of Life, the Abuse of Religion and the Scandals of Conversation. These Worshipful Things are the *Poets* Favourites: They appear at the Head of the *Fashion*; and shine in Character, and Equipage. If there is any Sense stirring, They must have it, tho' the rest of the *Stage* suffer never so much by the Partiality. And what can be the Meaning of this wretched Distribution of Honour? Is it not to give Credit and Countenance to Vice, and to shame young People out of all pretences to Conscience, and Regularity? They seem forc'd to turn Lewd in their own Defence: They can't otherwise justifie themselves to the Fashion, nor keep up the Character of Gentlemen: Thus People not well furnish'd with Thought, and Experience, are debauch'd both in Practise and Principle.

But even here Collier ruins his point by a blanket condemnation and by the examples he chooses. He does not mention one of the

[1] But not as much as Collier pretends. As Congreve wittily remarked: 'Mr *Collier*, in the high Vigour of his Obscenity, first commits a Rape upon my Words, and then arraigns 'em of Immodesty'.
[2] ibid., pp. 144–5.

heroes of Etherege or Otway to whom his strictures might apply.
Instead he lists the innocent Harcourt in *The Country Wife*, Mellefont
in *The Double Dealer* and Valentine in *Love for Love*, about whom
he is particularly sarcastic:[1]

This Spark the *Poet* would pass for a Person of Virtue, but he speaks too
late. 'Tis true, He was hearty in his Affection to *Angelica*. Now without
question, to be in Love with a fine Lady of 30,000 Pounds is a great Virtue!
But then abating this single Commendation, *Valentine* is altogether com-
pounded of Vice. He is a prodigal Debauchee, unnatural, and Profane,
Obscene, Sawcy, and undutiful, And yet this Libertine is crown'd for
the Man of Merit, has his Wishes thrown into his Lap, and makes the
Happy *Exit*. I perceive we should have a rare set of *Virtues* if these *Poets*
has the making of them! How they hug a Vitious Character, and how
profuse are they in their Liberalities to Lewdness!

Congreve had no difficulty in showing that Collier had been guilty
of gross distortion:[2]

Valentine is in *Debt*, and in *Love*; he has honesty enough to close with a
hard Bargain, rather than not pay his Debts, in the first *Act*; and he has
Generosity and Sincerity enough, in the last *Act*, to sacrifice every thing
to his Love; and when he is in danger of losing his Mistress, thinks every
thing else of little worth. This, I hope, may be allow'd a Reason for the
Lady to say, He has *Vertues*: They are such in respect to her; and her once
saying so, in the last *Act*, is all the notice that is taken of his *Vertue* quite
thro' the Play.
    Mr *Collier* says, he is *Prodigal*. He was Prodigal, and is shewn, in the
first *Act* under hard Circumstances, which are the Effects of his Prodigality.
. . . In short the Character is a mix'd Character; his Faults are fewer than
his good Qualities; and, as the World goes, he may pass well enough for
the best Character in a Comedy; where even the best must be shewn to
have Faults, that the best Spectators may be warn'd not to think too well
of themselves.

Yet it is true that the gallants, being handsome, gay and witty, are
treated sympathetically, and they appeal to the audience more than
the respectable people they outwit.
    It is difficult to understand how Macaulay could speak of Collier's
book in the terms he uses.[3]

[1] ibid., pp. 142–3.
[2] op. cit., pp. 452–3.
[3] *Critical and Historical Essays*, II (1907), p. 443.

There is hardly any book of that time from which it would be possible to select specimens of writing so excellent and so various . . . he was complete master of the rhetoric of honest indignation. We scarcely know any volume which contains so many bursts of that peculiar eloquence which comes from the heart and goes to the heart. Indeed the spirit of the book is truly heroic.

Macaulay was so convinced that Restoration comedy was 'a disgrace to our language and our national character', so certain that it was 'earthly, sensual, devilish' that he welcomed any opponent of it in extravagant terms.

   Macaulay's essay was written in 1841 when the plays of Wycherley and Congreve had long been banished from the stage. In the course of it he attacked Charles Lamb for his essay 'On the Artificial Comedy of the Last Century'; and much as we may deplore the ugly philistinism of Macaulay's views on the dramatists, he was in one important respect nearer the truth than Lamb had been. For the gentle Elia, anxious to reconcile his enjoyment of the plays of Wycherley and Congreve with the moral disapproval of his contemporaries, confessed that he was 'glad for a season to take an airing beyond the diocese of the strict conscience'. Restoration comedies[1]

are a world of themselves almost as much as fairy land. Take one of their characters, male or female (with few exceptions they are alike), and place it in a modern play, and my virtuous indignation shall rise against the profligate wretch as warmly as the Catos of the pit could desire; because in a modern play I am to judge of right and wrong . . . The Fainalls and the Mirabels, the Dorimants and the Lady Touchwoods, in their own sphere, do not offend my moral sense; in fact, they do not appeal to it at all. They seem engaged in their proper element. They break through no laws or conscientious restrains. They know of none. They have got out of Christendom into the land—what shall I call it?—of cuckoldry—the Utopia of gallantry, where pleasure is duty, and the manners perfect freedom. It is altogether a speculative scene of things, which has no reference whatever to the world that is.

   To this Macaulay retorted that in the world of Restoration comedy 'the garb, the manners, the topics of conversation are those of the real town and of the passing day'; the immorality depicted there 'is of a sort which can never be out of date'; that it is not true that no moral enters into these plays:

Morality constantly enters into that world, a sound morality, and an

[1] *The Essays of Elia* (ed. 1922), pp. 198–9.

unsound morality; the sound morality to be insulted, derided, associated
with everything mean and hateful; the unsound morality to be set off to
every advantage, and inculcated by all methods, direct and indirect.

Every person 'of narrow understanding and disgusting manners'
reverences sacred institutions and family ties. But the heroes and
heroines have an exceedingly bad code of morals:

The morality of the *Country Wife* and the *Old Bachelor* is the morality, not,
as Mr Charles Lamb maintains of an unreal world, but of a world which
is a great deal too real.

It is, of course, true that Restoration comedies depict the real
world, not an imaginary one. But we may suspect that Macaulay has
not properly understood Lamb's point. It is impossible to believe
that Lamb supposed that the world of the comedies was totally
unreal. He was merely saying, in an oblique manner, that even
though Wycherley and Congreve gave a faithful picture of the
society of their time, it was possible for a nineteenth-century gentleman to watch their plays without being harmed by them, because
of the antiseptic properties of time. He could laugh at the utopia
of gallantry, without having his own morals corrupted or under-
mined. Macaulay more or less admits this in his opening paragraphs
where he declares that, 'in a world so full of temptation as this',
it is difficult to believe that anyone has been corrupted by reading
Aristophanes or Juvenal, or more obscene classical authors.
     On one point Macaulay is quite wrong. To say that Fondlewife
and Pinchwife are the upholders of sound morality is to ignore their
characters. Pinchwife, for example, after leading the life of a rake,
marries an ignorant country girl because he could never keep a
whore to himself. One presumes that even Macaulay would hesitate
before claiming that this represented sound morality. As John
Palmer says:[1]

The anxieties of the ridiculous husbands in the plays of Wycherley and his
contemporaries are not the anxieties of men of honour. They are the
anxieties of men of property—surely a legitimate subject for ridicule.

Between 1840 and the end of the nineteenth century, the predominant attitude to the Restoration dramatists was that of
Macaulay. The first signs of a change were the publication of the

---

[1] *The Comedy of Manners* (1913), pp. 129–30.

Mermaid editions of Dryden, Wycherley, Otway, Shadwell, Congreve, Vanbrugh and Farquhar—although some of the editors
showed a good deal of uneasiness on the moral question, and
although Congreve and Wycherley were prefixed with Macaulay's
hostile criticisms—and Meredith's *Essay on Comedy*. Meredith did
a service in placing Congreve in the true line of critical comedy,
even if he made the mistake of Lamb, Hunt and Macaulay of
stressing the heartlessness of the characters in the comedies of the
period.

John Palmer's pioneering book, *The Comedy of Manners* (1913),
prepared the way for the rehabilitation of the *genre*, and revivals of
the plays in the theatre, after the First World War. These would
not have been possible without the violent reaction against Victorian
prudery both in the theatre and outside it.

During the years when Nigel Playfair was reviving *The Way of
the World, The Old Bachelor, The Beaux' Stratagem* and *The Beggar's
Opera*, a number of editions of the major dramatists, and several
books on their comedies, were published. These included *Restoration
Comedy* by Bonamy Dobrée (1924), *Comedy and Conscience after
the Restoration* by Joseph Wood Krutch (1924) and *The Social
Mode of Restoration Comedy* by Kathleen M. Lynch (1926). These
books sought to place the comedy in relation to the social back-
ground, and to trace its ancestry. Dobrée argued that 'the distinguishing characteristic of Restoration comedy down to Congreve is
that it is concerned with the attempt to rationalise sexual relationships';[1] he also analysed the musical subtleties of Congreve's prose.
By the beginning of the 'thirties the comedy of manners had recovered
the critical reputation and the popularity it had not had for more
than two centuries, and in 1937 Virginia Woolf wrote the most
eloquent eulogy of Congreve.

In the same year, the reaction set in. L. C. Knights published a
damning indictment of the comedy of manners in *Scrutiny*. He complained of the mechanical and monotonous nature of Congreve's
prose, of the absence in the comedies of the period of the values
found in them by Professor Dobrée and Miss Lynch, of the fact
that 'in the matter of sexual relations Restoration comedy is entirely
dominated by a narrow set of conventions', of the lack of genuine
sexual feelings, of Millamant's lack of intelligence, and of the
superficial cynicism which is everywhere apparent. He concludes
with the ringing statement that 'the criticism that defenders of

[1] op. cit., p. 23.

Restoration comedy need to answer is not that the comedies are "immoral", but that they are trivial, gross and dull'.[1]

An attempt will be made in the course of this book to answer these criticisms. But Professor Knights' final challenge seems very odd. How can the Juvenalian savagery of Wycherley be regarded as trivial? How can the most civilised of all English dramatists be regarded as gross? How can anyone regard *The Country Wife* or *Love for Love* as dull? Knights is such a fine critic that one is driven to seek for some explanation when he shows imperfect sympathies. It may partly be that Bloomsbury's praise[2] of Congreve was regarded as an indication of his superficiality; and though Knights does not discuss the moral issue one suspects that his general disdain and disgust for Restoration comedy is ultimately a matter of morals. He has more in common with Collier and Macaulay than he is aware of.

John Wain in one of his *Preliminary Essays* (1957)—part of which had appeared in *Essays in Criticism*—referred to Knights' diatribe as the best treatment of the subject. His own view is scarcely more flattering, except that he seems to approve of *The Man of Mode* for its truth to life. He, like Knights, thinks that Congreve's prose has been overpraised, that Wycherley 'never achieved clarity on any basic issue', and that the only enjoyable parts of the plays are when the dramatists 'are writing speeches for their grotesques to utter'. Mr Wain's determination not to be impressed by Restoration comedy can best be seen in his remarks on Congreve's prose style:

Congreve had a good ear for idiosyncracies of speech, and knew how to write sentences that are short and rhythmical and sound well when spoken from the stage, but so did the author of *Charley's Aunt*.

If Mr Wain really thought that this does justice to Congreve's style, we should wonder whether he ought to discuss dramatic dialogue at all. But he is, presumably, merely expressing his irritation with Dobrée's 'curious overpraise of Congreve in terms of cadences, rhythmical balance and what-not'.

It is unfortunate that Mr Wain thinks it necessary to be so partisan for his essay opens with some interesting remarks about the relation

[1] *Explorations* (1946), pp. 131–49.
[2] e.g. by Lytton Strachey who, in *Portraits in Miniature* (1931), p. 49, spoke of Congreve's plays as 'among the most wonderful and glorious creations of the human mind'.

of Restoration comedy to the age in which it was written: that it reflects class interests, that it is one of the symptoms of a sick society, that it 'is part of the literature of the Civil War; it has all the animosity of the battlefield in its heart'.

This last point is taken up by F. W. Bateson in a reply to L. C. Knights (*Essays in Criticism*, 1957) when he writes:

. . . the relative sexual respectability of *The Tatler* and *The Spectator* was the end-product of a long process that was closely connected with political developments. If the political problem *par excellence* in the second half of the seventeenth century was to avoid the recurrence of a second Civil War, its social parallel, essentially, was to rationalise the sex instinct. Until such a rationalisation had been achieved genuine communication between Whigs and Tories was hardly possible. Inter-marriage, the final solution, was unthinkable. It is now a matter of history that a kind of sexual rationalisation was achieved . . . From one point of view, in the mode of allegory proper to high comedy, the Restoration drama records the strains that accompanied the achievement.

The idea that the comedy was concerned with the rationalisation of the sex instinct goes back to Dobrée. Certainly—despite Knights' view that it is entirely cerebral—it is the only branch of English comedy which is almost exclusively concerned with sexual relations, in and out of marriage. But it is important to stress that the dramatists reflected the manners and modes of society, as well as sought to alter them. Etherege is more or less contented with the existing situation; Dryden is tolerantly amused at it; and Wycherley lashes the crying age. By the time we get to Congreve—and to the reign of William and Mary—it was possible to make more subtle comments on love and marriage.

It is along such lines as these that the best comedies of the period may be defended from the charge of triviality, for the relationship of the sexes is the acid test of a civilisation:

The immediate, natural and necessary relation of one human being to another is that of man to woman. From the character of this relationship, it can be seen how far man has developed. The relation of man to woman is the most natural relation of one person to another: in it is revealed how far the natural behaviour of man has become human—how far his human nature has become for him his real nature. In this relationship, too, is revealed how far the needs of man have become human needs, that is to say, how far another person has become one of his needs as a human being—how far existence has become mutual being.

In the light of these remarks[1] by the young philosopher, Karl Marx, the years following the Restoration would have to be condemned as uncivilised. Woman to the gallant, both on and off the stage, was merely a sexual prey; and that the woman was likewise predatory, or at least a willing victim, does not make the relationship any more satisfactory. In this respect the puritans were more civilised than many of their opponents. But by the end of the period, whether because of middle-class pressure, or exhaustion, or rationality, there was a marked improvement: and this improvement was reflected in the comedies of Southerne and Congreve, who were the most sensitive of the dramatists, in whose plays the heroines were moral beings and not merely sexual objects.

It is nevertheless important not to pretend that the plays are propagandist. All comedy has a Saturnalian element. We sympathise with the riotous Sir Toby and laugh at the respectable Malvolio; with one side of our natures we prefer Falstaff to the Lord Chief Justice; and, in the comedy of many different literatures the prodigal is depicted more sympathetically than the usurer, the cuckolder than the cuckold, the wine-bibber than the total abstainer. So the audiences of the plays of Etherege and Congreve, both in their day and ours, even those whose sexual morals are beyond reproach, enjoy watching the outrageous behaviour of the rakes, and they enjoy listening to the breaking of verbal taboos. The respectable probably appreciate obscenity on the stage more than those who practise it, because of the greater sense of release they feel in escaping from the prison of their normal existence. To this extent, Lamb was right to recognise the enjoyment he received from taking 'an airing beyond the diocese of the strict conscience'.

It has been implied above that the various dramatists differ so widely from each other that to a critic the differences are more important than the resemblances. In the chapters which follow, therefore, each of the more important dramatists will be considered separately. This will have the advantage of reducing the temptation of attempting to make them all fit into a general theory—a weakness of one or two of the best books on the subject.

---

[1] cf. *Economic and Philosophic Manuscripts of 1844* (1958), p. 101, for a different translation from mine by M. Milligan.

2

SIR GEORGE ETHEREGE

Sir George Etherege was very much of an amateur. Not having to write for a living, and being indolent by nature, he wrote only three plays: but by means of these he obtained an extraordinary reputation. 'There is none', Rochester wrote, 'with more fancy, sense, judgment and wit'; Dryden said he would 'never enter the lists in prose with the undoubted best author of it which our nation has produced'; and Edward Phillips, Milton's nephew, remarked more soberly that 'for pleasant wit, and no bad economy', Etherege's plays were 'judged not unworthy the applause they have met with'.

It is often said that in his plays Restoration society was able to see itself presented on the stage for the first time, conversing in the language of the age. But in Etherege's earliest play, *The Comical Revenge; or Love in a Tub* (1664), there is little realistic dialogue. Dufoy speaks an absurd language thought appropriate to a French servant, and the comical revenge inflicted on him is, as Pepys complained, only merry 'by gesture, not wit at all, which methinks is beneath the house'. The aristocratic lovers—Beaufort, Bruce, Graciana and Aurelia—speak in feeble rhymed couplets. Some speeches are in blank verse. Only in the scenes in which Sir Frederick Frollick appears is there an approximation to the language of the age.[1] By the time Etherege overcame his natural indolence to write

[1] Jocelyn Powell (*Restoration Theatre*, pp. 43–69) defends *The Comical Revenge* because it 'contains elements of many forms of dramatic expression, blended together into something quite new'; because 'the handling of Sir Frederick's scenes is brilliant'; because of the juxtaposition of the grotesque and farcical with the elegant and witty; and because it 'should not be read as a comedy of manners that has failed, but as a comedy ballet'. This seems to me to be special

his second comedy, *She Wou'd if She Cou'd*, Dryden had written the
brilliant prose scenes of *Secret Love*.

Although *She Wou'd if She Cou'd* is infinitely superior to Etherege's
first play, it was not at first as successful. Pepys, on the first night,
heard the author blame the actors 'that they were out of humour,
and had not their parts perfect, and that Harris [who played Sir
Joslin Jolly] did do nothing, nor could so much as sing a ketch in it'.
But Shadwell said he had the authority of some of the best judges in
England to say that it was the best comedy since the Restoration—
as indeed it was—though as Mrs Shadwell played the part of Lady
Cockwood he may have been prejudiced.

Rochester said that Etherege 'writ two talking plays without one
plot', and certainly the plot is the weakest thing in *She Wou'd if She
Cou'd* as in *The Comical Revenge*. The path of true love runs
remarkably smoothly. As soon as the young men meet Ariana and
Gatty in Act II we know what the end will be; and the progress of
their courtship receives only a temporary set-back from the stratagem of the jealous Lady Cockwood. Some of the individual scenes
are excellent. When Mrs Sentry's mission from her mistress to
Courtall is interrupted by the unexpected arrival of Sir Oliver
Cockwood; or when the masked Lady Cockwood arrives at her
husband's party and he takes her for the wench he has been expecting;
or when Freeman and Courtall, both on a visit to Lady Cockwood,
hide in a closet and overhear Ariana and Gatty talking about them—
these examples show that Etherege had an admirable sense of the
stage.

The characters are generally well drawn—it is only the feebleness
of Sir Joslin's songs that make him a bit of a bore—and the dialogue
is easy and natural. Lady Cockwood, who has been called a female
Tartuffe, makes 'use of hypocrisy as a cloak for a single failing' as
Brett-Smith rightly says. But though she talks a great deal about the
honour she is secretly anxious to lose, and though she does some
stupid and some wicked things in the course of the play, she is not
denied all sympathy. It is made plain that her husband gives her

pleading. The play is a muddle rather than a harmonious blending and it is
mostly crude and flat rather than elegant and witty. Dale Underwood, however,
in *Etherege and the Seventeenth Century Comedy of Manners* (1957), p. 44, argues
that 'the work as a whole expresses a view and a purpose which can be shown . . .
to anticipate more precisely than any play before it the comedy found in the
later and major works of the period'. He goes on to say that 'the comic world of
the plays exists always within the larger world of conventionality' and that Sir
Frederick's attempt to seduce the widow and her insistence on marriage is a
situation which is repeated in many Restoration plays.

little sexual satisfaction and that he is unfaithful to her as often as possible, and it is also apparent that Courtall had led her to suppose he was willing to satisfy her desires, and he confesses to Freeman that his only objection to her is that she is 'foolishly fond and troublesome'. It is part of his masculine vanity that he likes to pursue and not to be pursued. As Freeman tells him: 'This is rather an aversion in thee, than any real fault in the Woman'. So that Lady Cockwood's pretences are not so much deliberate hypocrisy as the camouflage of a desperate and frustrated woman. This is made clear by her soliloquies and asides. When she finds that Courtall has broken an appointment with her to keep one with another woman, she tells her maid not to be concerned for her as she has conquered her affection for Courtall; but as soon as she is alone, she bursts out:

> How am I fill'd with indignation! To find my person and my passion both despis'd, and what is more, so much precious time fool'd away in fruitless expectation.

But effective as the portrait of Lady Cockwood is, Etherege's greatest success is in the depiction of the four young lovers, and especially of the women. Courtall and Freeman, described without irony as 'Two honest Gentlemen of the Town', are frank hedonists on the look-out for sexual adventures. They decide to get acquainted with Ariana and Gatty because they happen to be without mistresses for the moment:

> Well, since there is but little ready money stirring, rather than want entertainment, I shall be contented to play a while upon Tick.

Courtall tells Freeman that

> a single intrigue in Love is as dull as a single Plot in a Play, and will tire a Lover worse, than t'other does an Audience.

They both begin with the assumption that marriage is a misfortune which they will avoid at all costs. They are almost inclined to agree with Sir Oliver who exclaims: 'Well, a pox of this tying man and woman together, for better, for worse!' Freeman explains the rude things Sir Oliver says about his wife by telling her: 'If you did but know, Madam, what an odious thing it is to be thought to live a Wife in good Company, you wou'd easily forgive him'. Courtall, when he first encounters the masked Gatty, tells her:

Now would not I see thy face for the world; if it should but be half so good as thy humour, thou woud'st dangerously tempt me to doat upon thee, and forgetting all shame, become constant.

And, near the end of the play, Ariana tells the men:

I know you wou'd think it as a great a Scandal to be thought to have an inclination for Marriage, as we shou'd to be believ'd willing to take our freedom without it.

Like so many heroes of Restoration comedies, the rakes are converted to the idea of matrimony by meeting with two attractive girls who will not surrender without. Of course, the attraction of Ariana and Gatty, two girls up from the country, is not merely physical. They are both more than a match for the men in their wit-combats and they are as anxious for adventures, within strictly defined limits. What those limits are can be seen from their dialogue in the second scene of the play. It will be observed that the two girls are well differentiated, and they live up to their Uncle's nicknames for them—Sly-girl for Ariana and Mad-cap for Gatty:

Gat. My dear Ariana, how glad am I we are in this Town again.
Ari. But we have left the benefit of the fresh Air, and the delight of wandering in the pleasant Groves.
Gat. Very pretty things for a young Gentlewoman to bemoan the loss of indeed, that's newly come to a relish of the good things of this world.
Ari. Very good, Sister!
Gat. Why, hast not thou promis'd me a thousand times, to leave off this demureness?
Ari. But you are so quick.
Gat. Why, wou'd it not make any one mad to hear thee bewail the loss of the Country? speak but one grave word more, and it shall be my daily Prayers thou may'st have a jealous Husband, and then you'le have enough of it I warrant you.
Ari. It may be, if your tongue be not altogether so nimble, I may be conformable; But I hope you do not intend we shall play such mad Reaks as we did last Summer?
Gat. 'Slife, do'st thou think we come here to be mew'd up, and take only the liberty of going from our Chamber to the Dining-Room, and from the Dining-Room to our Chamber again? and like a Bird in a Cage, with two Perches only, to hop up and down, up and down?
Ari. Well, thou art a mad Wench.
Gat. Would'st thou never have us go to a Play but with our grave Relations, never take the air but with our grave Relations? to feed their

pride, and make the world believe it is in their power to afford some
Gallant or other a good bargain?

Ari. But I am afraid we shall be known again.

Gat. Pish! the men were only acquainted with our Vizards and our
Petticoats, and they wore out long since: how I envy that Sex! Well!
we cannot plague 'em enough when we have it in our power for those
privileges which custom has allowed 'em above us.

Ari. The truth is, they can run and ramble here, and there, and every
where, and we poor Fools rather think the better of 'em.

Gat. From one Play-house, to the other Play-house, and if they like
neither the Play nor the Women, they seldom stay any longer than
the combing of their Perriwigs, or a whisper or two with a Friend;
and then they cock their Caps, and out they strut again.

Ari. But whatsoever we do, prithee now let us resolve to be mighty honest.

Gat. There I agree with thee.

Ari. And if we find the Gallants like lawless Subjects, who the more their
Princes grant, the more they impudently crave—

Gat. We'll become absolute Tyrants, and deprive 'em of all the priviledges
we gave 'em.

Ari. Upon these conditions I am contented to trail a Pike under thee—
march along, Girl.

At the end of the play, when the men are about to surrender,
Gatty says mockingly: 'I hope you are not in so desperate a condition
as to have a good opinion of Marriage, are you?' And Ariana adds:
' 'Tis to as little purpose to treat with us of anything under that, as
it is for those kind Ladies, that have obliged you with a valuable
consideration, to challenge the performance of your promise'. It
is Etherege's triumph to make us believe in the erosion of the gallants'
libertinism by the mockery and flouting to which they are submitted
by the ladies. The dramatist was very far from having a didactic
purpose but he reflected very accurately the life around him. The
young lovers who embark on matrimony at the end of the play
have the chance of avoiding shipwreck because they are fully aware
of the dangers; and the gallants may have reached the end of their
promiscuous phase.

The Man of Mode, or Sir Fopling Flutter (1676), Etherege's
masterpiece, came at the end of eight years' silence, and it was
immediately contemporary with Wycherley's last play, *The Plain
Dealer*. The fop, though an amusing character, is only on the periphery of the plot.[1] His function in that is merely to be used by Mrs
Loveit when she wants to spite Dorimant. He arrives 'piping hot

[1] He owes something to Wycherley's M. de Paris in *The Gentleman Dancing-
Master*.

from Paris'; he is 'the pattern of modern Foppery'; he affects a lisp 'in imitation of the people of Quality of France'; and, as Dorimant says, he is a person 'of great acquir'd Follies'. Mrs Loveit's stratagem is, in its way, successful, for Dorimant is made jealous; but he is enraged by the fear that he will be laughed at because of Mrs Loveit's choice, and he treats his former mistress with calculated rudeness. Mrs Loveit defends her flirting with Sir Fopling on the grounds that fools 'really admire us, while you at best but flatter us well'.

Dor. Take heed! Fools can dissemble too—
Love. They may! but not so artificially as you—There is no fear they
    should deceive us! Then they are assiduous, Sir, they are ever offering
    us their service, and always waiting on our will.
Dor. You owe that to their excessive idleness! They know not how to
    entertain themselves at home, and find so little welcome abroad,
    they are fain to fly to you who countenance 'em, as a refuge against
    the solitude they would be otherwise condemn'd to.
Love. Their conversation too diverts us better.
Dor. Playing with your Fan, smelling to your Gloves, commending your,
    Hair . . .[1]

Sir Fopling is the man of mode, as the title of the play makes clear. But it is possible that Etherege intended us to think that Dorimant was also, in his way, a man of mode[2]—a fashionable gallant, elegant, care-free and promiscuous. He is said to be based on Rochester: Etherege, we are told, wrote

Dorimant in Sir Fopling, in compliment to him, as drawing his Lordship's character, and burnishing all the Foibles of it, to make them shine like Perfections.

Dennis mentions various traits shared by Rochester and Dorimant—his wit, his amorous temper, his inconstancy, his 'Manner of his chiding his Servants' and 'his repeating, on every occasion, the Verses of *Waller*'.[3] Dorimant quotes from Waller eight times in the course of the play (and he also quotes passages by Suckling and Royden), and this helps to suggest that he is a man of taste as well as a man of mode. The last quotation is the most interesting.

[1] cf. *The Way of the World*, II.
[2] The point is made by N. N. Holland, *The First Modern Comedies*, pp. 87–8. Sexual success is 'an alternative kind of affectation'.
[3] *Critical Works* (1943), Vol. 2, p. 248.

B

Dorimant enters after his own song has been sung for Harriet and quotes from Waller the line

> Musick so softens and disarms the mind.

Harriet completes the couplet:

> That not one Arrow does resistance find.

This is one way of showing that Dorimant and Harriet are suited to each other. Mirabell's scene with Millamant in Act IV of *The Way of the World* opens in the same way with one of Waller's couplets shared between the two lovers. The fact that while Harriet also quotes from Cowley's *Davideis*, we cannot imagine Bellinda or Mrs Loveit being familiar with poetry, is an indication that Dorimant's relationship with Harriet has more chance of becoming permanent.

Dorimant's treatment of Mrs Loveit and Bellinda seems heartless to a modern reader or spectator, and it is usually assumed that the audience in 1676 would have felt differently about it. Dorimant 'pass'd for a fine Gentleman with the Court of King *Charles* the Second'.[1] Mrs Loveit, by wishing to keep hold of Dorimant after he had ceased to desire her, was breaking the unwritten laws of civilised conduct and deserved to suffer; so that even the good-natured Harriet can jeer at her without losing the admiration of the audience:

Love. Take example from my misfortunes, *Bellinda*; if thou would'st be happy, give thy self wholly up to goodness.
Har. Mr Dorimant has been your God Almighty long enough, 'tis time to think of another—

As for Bellinda, she surrendered to Dorimant too easily for him to value her. Under the double-standard everywhere apparent in the society of the time, as well as in its comedies, a woman who indulged in sexual intercourse before marriage, however desirable as a mistress, was not regarded as a suitable bride for a man of sense.

But are we meant to accept Dorimant's behaviour so easily? Steele, writing a generation later,[2] when society had changed a great deal, naturally complained of Dorimant's 'falsehood to Mrs Loveit,

---

[1] J. Dennis, op. cit., p. 244.
[2] *The Spectator*, No. 65.

Dorimant enters after his own song has been sung for Harriet and quotes from Waller the line

> Musick so softens and disarms the mind.

Harriet completes the couplet:

> That not one Arrow does resistance find.

This is one way of showing that Dorimant and Harriet are suited to each other. Mirabell's scene with Millamant in Act IV of *The Way of the World* opens in the same way with one of Waller's couplets shared between the two lovers. The fact that while Harriet also quotes from Cowley's *Davideis*, we cannot imagine Bellinda or Mrs Loveit being familiar with poetry, is an indication that Dorimant's relationship with Harriet has more chance of becoming permanent.

Dorimant's treatment of Mrs Loveit and Bellinda seems heartless to a modern reader or spectator, and it is usually assumed that the audience in 1676 would have felt differently about it. Dorimant 'pass'd for a fine Gentleman with the Court of King *Charles* the Second'.[1] Mrs Loveit, by wishing to keep hold of Dorimant after he had ceased to desire her, was breaking the unwritten laws of civilised conduct and deserved to suffer; so that even the good-natured Harriet can jeer at her without losing the admiration of the audience:

> *Love.* Take example from my misfortunes, *Bellinda*; if thou would'st be happy, give thy self wholly up to goodness.
> *Har. Mr Dorimant* has been your God Almighty long enough, 'tis time to think of another—

As for Bellinda, she surrendered to Dorimant too easily for him to value her. Under the double-standard everywhere apparent in the society of the time, as well as in its comedies, a woman who indulged in sexual intercourse before marriage, however desirable as a mistress, was not regarded as a suitable bride for a man of sense. But are we meant to accept Dorimant's behaviour so easily? Steele, writing a generation later,[2] when society had changed a great deal, naturally complained of Dorimant's 'falsehood to Mrs Loveit,

[1] J. Dennis, op. cit., p. 244.
[2] *The Spectator*, No. 65.

> Now would not I see thy face for the world; if it should but be half so good as thy humour, thou woud'st dangerously tempt me to doat upon thee, and forgetting all shame, become constant.

And, near the end of the play, Ariana tells the men:

> I know you wou'd think it as a great a Scandal to be thought to have an inclination for Marriage, as we shou'd to be believ'd willing to take our freedom without it.

Like so many heroes of Restoration comedies, the rakes are converted to the idea of matrimony by meeting with two attractive girls who will not surrender without. Of course, the attraction of Ariana and Gatty, two girls up from the country, is not merely physical. They are both more than a match for the men in their wit-combats and they are as anxious for adventures, within strictly defined limits. What those limits are can be seen from their dialogue in the second scene of the play. It will be observed that the two girls are well differentiated, and they live up to their Uncle's nicknames for them—Sly-girl for Ariana and Mad-cap for Gatty:

> *Gat.* My dear Ariana, how glad am I we are in this Town again.
> *Ari.* But we have left the benefit of the fresh Air, and the delight of wandering in the pleasant Groves.
> *Gat.* Very pretty things for a young Gentlewoman to bemoan the loss of indeed, that's newly come to a relish of the good things of this world.
> *Ari.* Very good, Sister!
> *Gat.* Why, hast not thou promis'd me a thousand times, to leave off this demureness?
> *Ari.* But you are so quick.
> *Gat.* Why, wou'd it not make any one mad to hear thee bewail the loss of the Country? speak but one grave word more, and it shall be my daily Prayers thou may'st have a jealous Husband, and then you'le have enough of it I warrant you.
> *Ari.* It may be, if your tongue be not altogether so nimble, I may be conformable; But I hope you do not intend we shall play such mad Reaks as we did last Summer?
> *Gat.* 'Slife, do'st thou think we come here to be mew'd up, and take only the liberty of going from our Chamber to the Dining-Room, and from the Dining-Room to our Chamber again? and like a Bird in a Cage, with two Perches only, to hop up and down, up and down?
> *Ari.* Well, thou art a mad Wench.
> *Gat.* Would'st thou never have us go to a Play but with our grave Relations, never take the air but with our grave Relations? to feed their

Ari. But I am afraid we shall be known again.

Gat. Pish! the men were only acquainted with our Vizards and our Petticoats, and they wore out long since: how I envy that Sex! Well! we cannot plague 'em enough when we have it in our power for those priviledges which custom has allowed 'em above us.

Ari. The truth is, they can run and ramble here, and there, and every where, and we poor Fools rather think the better of 'em.

Gat. From one Play-house, to the other Play-house, and if they like neither the Play nor the Women, they seldom stay any longer than the combing of their Perriwigs, or a whisper or two with a Friend; and then they cock their Caps, and out they strut again.

Ari. But whatsoever we do, prithee now let us resolve to be mighty honest.

Gat. There I agree with thee.

Ari. And if we find the Gallants like lawless Subjects, who the more their Princes grant, the more they impudently crave—

Gat. We'll become absolute Tyrants, and deprive 'em of all the priviledges we gave 'em.

Ari. Upon these conditions I am contented to trail a Pike under thee— march along, Girl.

At the end of the play, when the men are about to surrender, Gatty says mockingly: 'I hope you are not in so desperate a condition as to have a good opinion of Marriage, are you?' And Ariana adds: ' 'Tis to as little purpose to treat with us of anything under that, as it is for those kind Ladies, that have obliged you with a valuable consideration, to challenge the performance of your promise'. It is Etherege's triumph to make us believe in the erosion of the gallants' libertinism by the mockery and flouting to which they are submitted by the ladies. The dramatist was very far from having a didactic purpose but he reflected very accurately the life around him. The young lovers who embark on matrimony at the end of the play have the chance of avoiding shipwreck because they are fully aware of the dangers; and the gallants may have reached the end of their promiscuous phase.

The Man of Mode, or Sir Fopling Flutter (1676), Etherege's masterpiece, came at the end of eight years' silence, and it was immediately contemporary with Wycherley's last play, *The Plain Dealer*. The fop, though an amusing character, is only on the periphery of the plot.[1] His function in that is merely to be used by Mrs Loveit when she wants to spite Dorimant. He arrives 'piping hot

[1] He owes something to Wycherley's M. de Paris in *The Gentleman Dancing-Master*.

from Paris'; he is 'the pattern of modern Foppery'; he affects a lisp 'in imitation of the people of Quality of France'; and, as Dorimant says, he is a person 'of great acquir'd Follies'. Mrs Loveit's stratagem is, in its way, successful, for Dorimant is made jealous; but he is enraged by the fear that he will be laughed at because of Mrs Loveit's choice, and he treats his former mistress with calculated rudeness. Mrs Loveit defends her flirting with Sir Fopling on the grounds that fools 'really admire us, while you at best but flatter us well'.

> *Dor.* Take heed! Fools can dissemble too—
> *Love.* They may! but not so artificially as you—There is no fear they should deceive us! Then they are assiduous, Sir, they are ever offering us their service, and always waiting on our will.
> *Dor.* You owe that to their excessive idleness! They know not how to entertain themselves at home, and find so little welcome abroad, they are fain to fly to you who countenance 'em, as a refuge against the solitude they would be otherwise condemn'd to.
> *Love.* Their conversation too diverts us better.
> *Dor.* Playing with your Fan, smelling to your Gloves, commending your Hair . . .[1]

Sir Fopling is the man of mode, as the title of the play makes clear. But it is possible that Etherege intended us to think that Dorimant was also, in his way, a man of mode[2]—a fashionable gallant, elegant, care-free and promiscuous. He is said to be based on Rochester: Etherege, we are told, wrote

> Dorimant in Sir Fopling, in compliment to him, as drawing his Lordship's character, and burnishing all the Foibles of it, to make them shine like Perfections.

Dennis mentions various traits shared by Rochester and Dorimant— his wit, his amorous temper, his inconstancy, his 'Manner of his chiding his Servants' and 'his repeating, on every occasion, the Verses of *Waller*'.[3] Dorimant quotes from Waller eight times in the course of the play (and he also quotes passages by Suckling and Royden), and this helps to suggest that he is a man of taste as well as a man of mode. The last quotation is the most interesting.

[1] cf. *The Way of the World*, II.
[2] The point is made by N. N. Holland, *The First Modern Comedies*, pp. 87–8 Sexual success is 'an alternative kind of affectation'.
[3] *Critical Works* (1943), Vol. 2, p. 248.

B

and the barbarity of triumphing over her anguish for losing him'. Dennis, replying to Steele, argued[1] that Etherege

was oblig'd to accommodate himself to the Notion of a fine Gentleman, which the Court and the Town both had at the Time of the writing of this Comedy.

The best judges, moreover, have rightly believed

that the Characters, and especially the principal Characters, are admirably drawn, to answer the two Ends of Comedy, Pleasure and Instruction; and that the Dialogue is the most charming that has been writ by the Moderns: That with Purity and Simplicity, it has Art and Elegance; and with Force and Vivacity, the utmost Grace and Delicacy.

Nevertheless, Dennis denied that the characters are presented for our imitation, as Steele's own heroes were:

How little do they know of the Nature of true Comedy, who believe that its proper Business is to set us Patterns for Imitation: For all such Patterns are serious Things, and Laughter is the Life, and the very Soul of Comedy. 'Tis its proper Business to expose Persons to our View, whose Views we may spurn, and whose Follies we may despise; and by shewing us what is done upon the Comick Stage, to shew us what ought never to be done upon the Stage of the World.

Despite Steele and some more recent critics it is difficult to believe that even the fine gentlemen in Etherege's original audience would accept Dorimant's conduct as worthy of imitation. As Dennis says, he

is a young Courtier, haughty, vain, and prone to Anger, amorous, false, and inconstant. He debauches *Loveit*, and betrays her; loves *Belinda*, and as soon as he enjoys her is false to her.

The character therefore instructs the audience

by his Insulting, and his Perfidiousness, and *Loveit* by the Violence of her Resentment and her Anguish. For *Loveit* has Youth, Beauty, Quality, Wit, and Spirit. And it was depending upon these, that she repos'd so dangerous a Trust in *Dorimont* [*sic*], which is a just Caution to the Fair Sex, never to be so conceited of the Power of their Charms, or their other extraordinary Qualities, as to believe they can engage a Man to be true to them, to whom they grant the best Favour,

[1] Dennis, op. cit., pp. 243 ff.

without the only sure Engagement, without which they can never be
certain, that they shall not be hated and despis'd by that very Person
whom they have done every Thing to oblige.

Dennis's argument is supported by the text of the play. In the first
scene Dorimant callously prophesies what Mrs Loveit's behaviour
will be:

She means insensibly to insinuate a Discourse of Me, and artificially
raise her Jealousie to such a height, that transported with the first
Motions of her Passion, she shall fly upon me with all the Fury
imaginable, as soon as ever I enter; the Quarrel being thus happily
begun, I am to play my Part, confess and justify all my Roguery,
swear her Impertinence and ill Humour makes her intolerable, tax
her with the next Fop that comes into my Head, and in a Huff march
away; slight her, and leave her to be taken by whosoever thinks it
worth his time to lye down before her.

He tells Medley that 'next to the coming to a good understanding
with a new Mistress', he loves 'a quarrel with an old one'. In the
second scene of Act II we find him indulging in this sadistic pleasure:

Love. Is this the Constancy you vowed?
Dor. Constancy at my years! 'tis not a virtue in season, you might as well
expect the Fruit the Autumn ripens i' the Spring . . . Youth has a long
Journey to go, Madam, should I have set up my rest at the first Inn I
lodged at, I should never have arrived at the happiness I now enjoy.
Love. Dissembler, damned Dissembler.
Dor. I am so, I confess; good Nature and good Manners corrupt me. I am
honest in my Inclinations, and would not, were't not to avoid
Offence . . . seem as fond of a thing I am weary of, as when I doated
on't in earnest.
Love. Think on your Oaths, your Vows and Protestations, perjured man.
Dor. I made 'em when I was in love.
Love. And therefore ought they not to bind? Oh, impious.
Dor. What we swear at such a time may be a certain Proof of a present
Passion; but to say Truth, in Love there is no security to be given for
the future.

The truth of this last remark does not excuse Dorimant's cruelty.
Bellinda deserves less sympathy. She enters into the intrigue with
her eyes open; she betrays her friend, Mrs Loveit; and she knows how
Dorimant treats his cast-off mistresses:

I knew him false, and help'd to make him so!
Was not her ruine enough to fright me from the danger?
It should have been, but love can take no warning.

Even if we attempt to excuse Dorimant's treatment of Mrs Loveit by the manners of the age—and the contemporary evidence is that Rochester's foibles were made to shine like perfections—there are several passages in the play where Dorimant is at a loss. He is very much embarassed by Mrs Loveit's encouragement of Sir Fopling and his attempted revenge is foiled. He is reduced to calling Mrs Loveit 'false woman', though all the falsity has been on his side, and the sight of Bellinda, who arrives at this moment, completes his discomfiture, as he had sworn to have nothing more to do with Mrs Loveit.

Bell. [*Aside*] He starts! and looks pale, the sight of me has touch his guilty soul.

Dorimant confesses he was never 'at such a loss before'.

Bell. One who makes a publick profession of breach of faith and Ingratitude! I loath the sight of him.
Dor. There is no remedy. I must submit to their Tongues now, and some other time bring my self off as well as I can.
Bell. Other men are wicked, but then they have some sense of shame! he is never well but when he triumphs, nay! glories to a Womans face in his Villanies. . .
Dor. You have reproach't me handsomely, and I deserve it for coming hither, but—
Pert. You must expect it, Sir! all Women will hate you for my Ladies sake!
Dor. Nay, if she begins too, 'tis time to fly! I shall be scolded to death else. [*Aside to* Bellinda] I am to blame in some circumstances I confess; but as to the Main, I am not so guilty as you imagine. I shall seek a more convenient time to clear my self.
Love. Do it now! What impediments are here?

Dorimant is routed and, as the stage-direction puts it, he 'flings off'. When Mrs Loveit and Bellinda arrive in the middle of the final scene, Dorimant mutters: 'The Devil owes me a shame to day, and I think never will have done paying it'. His reputation is so bad that with Lady Woodvil he has to pretend to be Mr Courtage; he lies to Loveit and Bellinda about his motives for marrying; and in the end he is snubbed by Bellinda. Dorimant violates the code of a gentleman by kissing and telling, and by his falsehoods; and the perceptive Harriet realises that, despite his attractions, he is a poseur:

> He's agreeable and pleasant I must own, but he does so much affect being so, he displeases me.

Although Bellair says, with surprise, that he never heard Dorimant 'accus'd of affectation before', the accusation sticks.

It is fairly clear that Etherege was not holding up Dorimant as the portrait of a perfect, gentle l night; and despite some faint signs that Harriet has tamed him, we are left in doubt as to whether she will not regret the bargain.[1]

The last scene of the play shows Harriet concealing her genuine feeling—as Millamant was later to do—under a mask of flippancy:

Dor. 'Musick so softens and disarms the mind.'
Har. 'That not one Arrow does resistance find.'
Dor. Let us make use of the lucky Minute then.
Har. [*Aside*] My love springs with my blood into my Face. I dare not look upon him yet.
Dor. What have we here, the picture of a celebrated Beauty, giving Audience in publick to a declar'd Lover?
Har. Play the dying Fop, and make the piece compleat, Sir.
Dor. What think you if the Hint were well improv'd? The whole mystery of making love pleasantly designed and wrought in a suit of Hangings?
Har. 'Twere needless to execute fools in Effigie who suffer daily in their own persons.
Emil. ... Here are dreadful preparations, Mr. *Dorimant*, Writings sealing, and a Parson sent for—
Dor. To marry this Lady?
Emil. Condemn'd she is, and what will become of her I know not, without you generously engage in a Rescue.
Dor. In this sad condition, Madam, I can do no less than offer you my service.

---

[1] Thomas H. Fujimura, *The Restoration Comedy of Wit*, pp. 105, 116, declares that Dorimant 'is too often dismissed as a cruel and selfish rake; whereas he is actually a superb portrait of a Truewit'. Later, he says that Dorimant and Harriet 'represent the finest expression of Etherege's witty attitude towards life—his good sense, elegance and libertinism; and his scorn of fools, ceremony and artificiality'. He claims that the world of the Truewit contains much of value, 'elegance, intellectual distinction, clarity of thought, absence of artificial formality, freedom from cant about honor, and a graceful and natural acceptance of this life on earth.'

Har. The obligation is not great, you are the common sanctuary for all young Women who run from their Relations.

Dor. I have always my arms open to receive the distressed. But I will open my heart and receive you, where none yet did ever enter—You have fill'd it with a secret, might I but let you know it—

Har. Do not speak it, if you would have me believe it; your Tongue is so fam'd for falshood, 'twill do the truth an injury.

Dor. Turn not away then; but look on me and guess it.

Har. Did you not tell me there was no credit to be given to faces? that Women nowadays have their passions as much at will as they have their Complexions, and put on joy and sadness, scorn and kindness, with the same ease as they do their Paint and Patches—Are they the only counterfeits?

Dor. You wrong your own, while you suspect my Eyes; by all the hope I have in you, the inimitable colour in your cheeks is not more free from art than are the sighs I offer.

Har. In men who have been long harden'd in Sin, we have reason to mistrust the first signs of repentance.

Dor. The prospect of such a Heav'n will make me persevere, and give you marks that are infallible.

Har. What are those?

Dor. I will renounce all the joys I have in friendship and in Wine, sacrifice to you all the interest I have in other Women—

Har. Hold—Though I wish you devout, I would not have you turn Fanatick. Could you neglect these a while and make a journey into the Country?

Dor. To be with you I could live there; and never send one thought to *London.*

Har. Whate'er you say, I know all beyond *Hyde-Park's* a desert to you, and that no gallantry can draw you farther.

Dor. That has been the utmost limit of my Love—but now my passion knows no bounds, and there's no measure to be taken of what I'll do for you from any thing I ever did before.

Har. When I hear you talk thus in *Hampshire*, I shall begin to think there may be some little truth inlarged upon.

Dor. Is this all?—will you not promise me—?

Har. I hate to promise! What we do then is expected from us, and wants much of the welcom it finds, when it surprises.

Dor. May I not hope?

Har. That depends on you, and not on me, and 'tis to no purpose to forbid it.

Later on she asks him if he is prepared to come to a great rambling lone house, that looks as it were not inhabited, the family's so small; there you'l find my Mother, and old lame Aunt, and my self, Sir, perch'd up on Chairs at a distance in a large parlour; sitting moping like three or four Melancholy Birds in a spacious vollary—Does not this stagger your Resolution?

Dor. Not at all, Madam! The first time I saw you, you left me with the pangs of Love upon me, and this day my soul have has quite given up her liberty.

Har. This is more dismal than the Country, *Emilia!* pity me, who am going to that sad place. Methinks I hear the hateful noise of Rooks already—Kaw, Kaw, kaw. There's musick in the worst Cry in *London! My dill and Cowcumbers to pickle!*

Underwood calls *The Man of Mode* 'one of the masterpieces of English comedy'.[1] If it is not quite that, for the reasons suggested above, it is a very entertaining play and deserves to be revived more obviously than some Restoration comedies which have had considerable success on the modern stage. Horace Walpole goes further, in pointing out the historical importance of the play:[2]

The Man of Mode shines as our first genteel comedy; the touches are natural and delicate and never overcharged. Unfortunately the tone of the most fashionable people was extremely indelicate; and when Addison, in The Spectator, anathematised the play, he forgot that it was rather a satire on the manners of the court, than an apology for them. Less licentious conversation would not have painted the age.

[1] op. cit., p. 72.
[2] *Works*, Vol. 2, p. 315. *The Spectator* paper was, however, by Steele.

3

JOHN DRYDEN

Dryden wrote as many plays as Etherege, Wycherley, Congreve, Vanbrugh and Farquhar together. Altogether his plays—tragedies, comedies, tragi-comedies, adaptations from Shakespeare, libretti— covered a period of more than thirty years and three reigns. But despite his varied achievement in the dramatic form, and despite such masterpieces as *All for Love* and *Aureng-zebe*, Dryden's best work was not written for the stage. And since heroic drama is unlikely ever to be seen again in the theatre, one is almost tempted to say that the heroic verse of the plays was chiefly valuable as training —training for the couplets of *Absalom and Achitophel* and *The Hind and the Panther*.

Dryden had a low opinion of comedy and of his own talent for it: he wrote 'comedies rather than serious plays' simply in order to please the public.[1] He thought that he lacked 'that gaiety of humour' necessary for comedy'.[2]

My conversation is slow and dull; my humour saturnine and reserved; in short, I am none of those who endeavour to break jests in company, or make repartees. So that those, who decry my comedies, do me no injury, except it be in point of profit: reputation in them is the last thing to which I shall pretend.

It seems probable that the explanation of these views was his belief that farce was enjoyed by his audience as much as high comedy.

Dryden would, perhaps, have a greater reputation as a dramatist

[1] *Of Dramatic Poesy*, etc., Ed. G. Watson, I., p. 120.
[2] ibid. I., p. 116.

if we had the chance of seeing his plays on the stage. In recent years there have been revivals of *All for Love* and *Marriage à la Mode*, but not of any of the heroic plays or any of the other comedies. One difficulty is that some of Dryden's best comedy is to be found in plays which in other ways are less revivable. Dryden's earliest comedy, *The Wild Gallant* (1663), has little to recommend it; and four years elapsed before he returned to comic writing in *Secret Love*. The main plot, which is concerned with the queen's love for one of her subjects and her renouncement of it in the interests of 'glory', comes nearer, perhaps, to French classical tragedy than any play of the period. But its chief merit consists in the gaiety and wit of the comic scenes in which Florimell woos and wins the promiscuous Celadon. The two halves of the play are not unrelated. Celadon has an important function in the abortive rebellion against the queen; and, as John Loftis has pointed out,[1] 'there is a juxtaposition of love plots in different moods':

The plots reveal certain parallels of detail: dialogue in praise of the queen's beauty (I.iii) follows similar dialogue in praise of Florimell's (I.ii); depiction of the queen's jealousy and petulant criticism of her rival Candiope (III.i) precedes a similar depiction of Florimell's jealousy and criticism of her two rivals . . . (IV.i)

Although these observations are true, the fact remains that the Florimell–Celadon scenes are quite different in tone, a tone that was largely original and which was Dryden's great contribution to Restoration comedy.

Celadon and Florimell are early examples of what John Harrington Smith calls 'The Gay Couple' and their independence and their pretence of cynicism does not mean that they are not deeply in love with each other. Nell Gwyn's playing of the part of Florimell aroused Pepys' enthusiasm:

So great performance of a comical part was never, I believe, in the world before as Nell do this, both as a mad girle, then most and best of all when she comes in like a young gallant, and hath the motions and carriage of a spark the most that ever I saw any man have.

Celadon is the archetypal philanderer who makes love to every pretty woman but who thinks that 'Marriage is poor folks pleasure that cannot go to the cost of variety'. He tells Florimell:

[1] *The Works of John Dryden*, IX (1966), pp. 335–6.

Yet for my part, I can live with as few Mistresses as any man: I desire no superfluities; only for necessary change or so; as I shift my Linnen.

Florimell brings Celadon to the point of matrimony by her wit and gaiety, by her cunning tactics, by her acceptance of her lover's temperament, and by her refusal to accept him on easy terms. When it is pointed out that Celadon loves others, she retorts:

There's the more hope he may love me among the rest: hang't, I would not marry one of these solemn fops; They are good for nothing but to make Cuckolds: Give me a servant that is an high Flier at all games, that is bounteous of himself to many women; and yet whenever I pleas'd to throw out the lure of Matrimony, should come down with a swing, and fly the better at his own quarry.

Florimell adopts various stratagems. She imposes a year of probation, with an extension if Celadon proves unfaithful; she sends an invitation to him in the names of Melissa's daughters and catches him kissing one of them; she dresses as a man and lures both the girls from him; and finally agrees on conditions of marriage.

Flor. But this Marriage is such a Bugbear to me; much might be if we could invent but any way to make it easie.
Cel. Some foolish people have made it uneasie, by drawing the knot faster than they need, but we that are wiser will loosen it a little.
Flor. 'Tis true indeed, there's some difference betwixt a Girdle and an Halter.
Cel. As for the first year, according to the laudable custom of new married people, we shall follow one another up into chambers, and down into Gardens, and think we shall never have enough of one another.—So far 'tis pleasant enough I hope.
Flor. But after that, when we begin to live like Husband and Wife, and never come near one another—what then Sir?
Cel. Why, then our onely happiness must be, to have one mind, and one will, *Florimell.*
Flor. One mind, if thou wilt, but prithee let us have two wills; for I find one will be little enough for me alone: But how, if those wills should meet and clash, *Celadon*?
Cel. I warrant thee for that; Husbands and Wives keep their wills far enough asunder for ever meeting. One thing let us be sure to agree on, that is, never to be jealous.
Flor. No; but e'en love one another as long as we can; and confess the truth when we can love no longer.

Cel. When I have been at play, you shall never ask me what money I have lost.

Flor. When I have been abroad you shall never inquire who treated me.

Cel. *Item*, I will have the liberty to sleep all night, without your interrupting my repose for any evil design whatsoever.

Flor. *Item*, Then you shall bid me good night before you sleep.

Cel. Provided always, that whatever liberties we take with other people, we continue very honest to one another.

Flor. As far as will consist with a pleasant life.

Cel. Lastly, Whereas the names of Husband and Wife hold forth nothing but clashing and cloying, and dulness and faintness in their signification; they shall be abolish'd for ever betwixt us.

Flor. And instead of those, we will be married by the more agreeable names of Mistress and Gallant.

Cel. None of my privileges to be infring'd by thee, *Florimell*, under the penalty of a month of Fasting-nights.

Flor. None of my privileges to be infring'd by thee, *Celadon*, under the penalty of Cuckoldom.

Cel. Well, if it be my fortune to be made a Cuckold, I had rather thou shouldst make me one, than any one in *Sicily*; and, for my comfort I shall have thee oftner than any of thy servants.

Flor. La ye now, is not such a marriage as good as wenching, *Celadon*?

Cel. This is very good, but not so good, *Florimell*.

This passage looks forward to the bargain scene in *The Way of the World* a generation later. The spirit of the two scenes is almost identical, although Millamant is a more subtly-realised character, and more reluctant, than Florimell. The passage also looks back, as Kathleen Lynch was the first critic to notice,[1] to Honoré D'Urfé's *L'Astreé*, where Hylas and Stelle set down twelve conditions of marriage, of which the following are examples:

> That no one shall exercise over the other that sovereign authority which we say is tyranny.
>
> That each of us shall be at the same time both lover and beloved.
>
> That our friendship will be eternally without constraint.
>
> That we shall love as long as we please.
>
> That one can cease loving without any reproach of infidelity.
>
> That jealousy, complaints and sadness shall be banished from our midst as incompatible with our perfect friendship.

[1] *PQ*, IV (1925), pp. 302–8.

In order that we shall not be liars or slaves, words of fidelity, servitude, and of eternal affection shall never be used by us.

As *L'Astreé* was the chief source of *Secret Love* there is no reason to doubt that Dryden took the idea of conditions from this passage, but, as Frank H. Moore suggests,[1] the sustained banter of Celadon and Florimell may be modelled on that of Fletcher's lovers.

Since Fletcher's day the question of sexual relationships had become a matter of debate. Society, in reaction against the puritanical views of the previous age, had become more openly licentious than at any previous time; vows of eternal fidelity hardly seemed to square with the facts of life, and the Cavalier poets, no less than their successors after the Restoration, proclaimed that the satisfaction of desire was fatal to its continuance. Asteria's couplet, in one of the serious scenes of *Secret Love*, puts the matter neatly. She urges the queen to let Philocles marry:

> Let him possess, and then he'll soon repent:
> And so his crime will prove his punishment.

Dryden's later couple, Rhodophil and Doralice in *Marriage à la Mode*, have committed matrimony without taking the precautions of Celadon and Florimell who know that although they are in love and although they have similar tastes they cannot guarantee that their love will endure. But half the fun of their proviso scene, as of the one in *The Way of the World*, depends on the dichotomy between reason and emotion.

We may pass over *Sir Martin Mar-All*, performed in the same year as *Secret Love*, not because it seemed to L. C. Knights to be the stupidest play he had ever read, but because Dryden was merely revising a play by the Duke of Newcastle. *An Evening's Love* (1668) is one of the finest of Dryden's comedies. The dialogue is less brilliant than that of *Secret Love* or *Marriage à la Mode*, but in other respects it is superior to either; it has a clever plot and the scenes have a unity of tone—we are not made to oscillate between the heroic and the realistic, between verse and contemporary prose. The stratagem which gives the play its sub-title, *The Mock Astrologer*, though it strains our credulity, is theatrically effective; the disguisings of Jacinta—played, like Florimell, by Nell Gwyn—are gay and

---

[1] *The Nobler Pleasure* (1963), chapter III; and see Loftis' edition of the play, p. 343.

spirited; and, above all, the wit-combats of the lovers are second only to those in *Secret Love*.

The libertine sentiments professed by Wildblood are eroded in the course of the play. In the first scene he scoffs at the very idea of marriage:

> Marriage quoth a! what, dost thou think I have been bred in the Desarts of *Africk*, or among the Savages of America? nay, if I had, I must needs have known better things than so; the light of Nature would not have let me gone [go?] so far astray.

He tells Jacinta in the second scene:

> I beseech you, Madam, trouble not your self for my Religion; for though I am a Heretick to the men of your Country, to your Ladies I am a very zelous Catholick.

In II.1, Bellamy confesses that if a woman flies he feels bound to pursue, and Wildblood replies:

> What a secret have you found out? Why 'tis the nature of all mankind: we love to get our Mistresses, and purr over 'em, as Cats do over Mice, and then let 'em go a little way; and all the pleasure is, to pat 'em back again.

When Jacinta, who pretends to share his libertine views, proposes a short love affair, Wildblood agrees with alacrity:

> Faith agreed with all my heart. For I am none of those unreasonable lovers, that propose to themselves the loving to eternity; the truth is, a month is commonly my stint; but in that month I love so dreadfully; that it is after a twelve-month's rate of common love.
> *Jacinta* Or would not a fortnight serve our turn? for in troth a month looks somewhat dismally; 'tis a whole *Ægytpian* year.

Before the end of the play, Wildblood is desperately in love, and his quarrels with Jacinta are a proof of their mutual affection:

Wildblood Why, are we quite broke off?
Jacinta Why, are we not?
Wildblood Well, since 'tis past, 'tis past; but a pox of all foolish quarrelling for my part.
Jacinta And a mischief of all foolish disguisements for my part.
Wildblood But if it were to do again with another Mistress, I would e'en

plainly confess I had lost my money . . . If it were not to please you,
I see no necessity of our parting.
Jacinta I protest I do it out of complaisance to you.

Dryden is alleged to have called *An Evening's Love* 'but a fifth-rate
play' and he speaks of it in the Prologue as the result of 'ungrateful
drudgery'. He may have felt that it was a piece of hack writing,
based partly on Molière's *Le Dépit amoureux* and partly on Thomas
Corneille's *Le Feint Astrologue*. But he surely underestimated the
quality of the amalgam, and the admirable comic dialogue. It
certainly does not—at least in its published form—deserve the
complaints of bawdiness levelled against it by Pepys and Evelyn. 'It
afflicted me', wrote Evelyn, 'to see how the stage was degenerated
and polluted by the licentious times'.

Marriage à la Mode (1673) contains Dryden's finest comic scenes,
although these are set in a romantic framework reminiscent of
Cymbeline or *Philaster*. The different strains do not blend satis-
factorily, not because the comic scenes are in prose and the others
in verse, but because the former reflect the manners and morals of
Charles II's England and seem unrelated to the Sicily, seen through
literary eyes, depicted in the serious scenes. Dryden tries without
much conviction to unite the two plots by making the gallants of
the comedy of manners fight gallantly on behalf of the rightful
king. But their previous modishness hardly prepares us for Palamedes
ringing couplet:

> Or die with you: no Subject e'er can meet
> A nobler fate, than at his Sovereign's feet.

Shakespeare, of course, had successfully joined things even more
incompatible, filling a wood near Athens with English craftsmen, or
blending in *Cymbeline* folk-tale, pastoral, ancient history and
Renaissance Italy. But in both cases the poetry acts as a solvent. In
Dryden's play the quartet of lovers live in a different world from
that occupied by Polydamas, the usurper, Palmyra, his daughter,
and Leonidas, the rightful Prince. Both worlds, if considered
separately, are successfully presented; but the realism of the prose
scenes makes the poetical ones seem unreal.

The see-saw of events, which first reveals that Leonidas is the
king's son and so separates him from Palmyra, and then reveals that
Palmyra is the king's child and Leonidas is not, again separating the

lovers, and at last reveals that Leonidas is the rightful monarch, is an effective romantic vehicle. For full measure, there is another beautiful princess in love with Leonidas. Moreover the play contains some of Dryden's most charming verse, especially the lovers' remembrance of things past:

Leon. When Love did of my heart possession take,
   I was so young, my soul was scarce awake:
   I cannot tell when first I thought you fair;
   But suck'd in Love, insensibly as Ayre.
Palm. I know too well when first my love began,
   When at our Wake you for the chaplet ran:
   Then I was made the Lady of the May,
   And, with the Garland, at the Goal did stay:
   Still, as you ran, I kept you full in view;
   I hop'd, and wish'd, and ran, methought, for you.
   As you came near, I hastily did rise,
   And stretch'd my arm out-right, that held the prize.
   The custom was to kiss whom I should crown;
   You kneel'd and, in my lap, your head laid down:
   I blush'd, and blush'd, and did the kiss delay:
   At last, my Subjects forc'd me to obey;
   But, when I gave the crown, and then the kiss,
   I scarce had breath to say, Take that—and this.
Leon. I felt, the while, a pleasing kind of smart;
   That kiss went, tingling, to my very heart.
   When it was gone, the sense of it did stay;
   The sweetness cling'd upon my lips all day,
   Like drops of Honey, loath to fall away.
Palm. Life, like a prodigal, gave all his store
   To my first youth, and now can give no more.
   You are a Prince; and, in that high degree,
   No longer must converse with humble me.

With this pastoral idealism and the heroic fidelity it inspires, Dryden contrasts the fashionable assumptions about marriage of the society of his time, just as the adulteries and gallantries of the comedy of manners contrast with the inflated virtues and passions of heroic tragedy. Rhodophil and Doralice are out of love with each other not because they are ill-matched, like the Brutes and Sullens, but because they are married. The opening song states the theme: it might, indeed, be the theme-song for many Restoration comedies:

Why should a foolish Marriage Vow,
   Which long ago was made,
Oblige us to each other now,
   When Passion is decay'd?
We lov'd, and we lov'd, as long as we cou'd,
   Till our love was lov'd out in us both;
But our Marriage is dead, when the Pleasure is fled:
   'Twas Pleasure first made it an Oath.

If I have Pleasures for a Friend,
   And farther love in store,
What wrong has he, whose joys did end
   And who cou'd give no more?
'Tis a madness that he should be jealous of me,
   Or that I should bar him of another:
For all we can gain, is to give our selves pain,
   When neither can hinder the other.

Rhodophil admits to Palamede that he is unhappy, despite the fact that Doralice is young, gay and beautiful. Palamede replies, 'You dislike her for no other reason, but because she's your wife'. Rhodophil asks, 'And is not that enough?' and he continues with a contrast between his feelings and those he had two years ago:

All that I know of her perfections now, is only by memory. I remember, indeed, that about two years ago I lov'd her passionately; but those golden days are gone, *Palamede*: Yet I lov'd her a whole half year, double the natural term of any Mistress; and I think in my conscience I could have held out another quarter; but then the World began to laugh at me, and a certain shame of being out of fashion, seiz'd me. At last, we arriv'd at that point, that there was nothing left in us to make us new to one another. Yet still I set a good face upon the matter, and am infinite fond of her before company; but, when we are alone, we walk like Lions in a room; she one way, and I another: and we lie with our backs to each other, so far distant, as if the fashion of great Beds was only invented to keep Husband and Wife sufficiently asunder.

The key words in this speech are 'the World began to laugh at me'. Dryden is both recording and satirising the fashionable view of marriage. The scene in which Rhodophil and Doralice act out the antagonism which is expected of them is a good example of Dryden's style which for wit and polish had no rival until the advent of Congreve twenty years later:

Rho. Well, thou art the most provoking Wife!

Dor. Well, thou art the dullest Husband, thou art never to be provok'd.

Rho. I was never thought dull till I marry'd thee; and now thou hast made an old knife of me; thou hast whetted me so long, till I have no edge left.

Dor. I see you are in the Husbands fashion; you reserve all your good humours for your Mistresses, and keep your ill for your wives.

Rho. Prethee leave me to my own cogitations; I am thinking over all my sins, to find for which of them it was I marry'd thee.

Dor. Whatever your sin was, mine's the punishment.

Rho. My comfort is, thou art not immortal; and when that blessed, that divine day comes, of thy departure, I'm resolv'd I'll make one Holy-day more in the almanac for thy sake.

Dor. Ay, you had need make a Holy-day for me, for I am sure you have made me a Martyr.

It is curious, in the light of such a passage of dialogue, that Dryden believed he had little talent as a writer of comedy, since he had not the gift of repartee. Every one of these speeches proves the contrary.

Bruce King suggests that Palamede and Rhodophil have 'accepted the Hobbist view of life according to which man is a series of appetites seeking new sensations', though, as King points out, Hobbes never said that married love was an impossibility.[1] Dryden had, of course, read Hobbes; but the idea that desire is destroyed by its satisfaction was continually being expressed both by the Metaphysical poets and the cavaliers, many of whom wrote before Hobbes published anything.

Dryden in his early plays seems to express, and even share, libertinist views of sexual behaviour; but in *Marriage à la Mode* not merely are the prose characters placed in opposition to the poetic characters (to whom love, fidelity and heroism are meaningful), but the gallants (and their mistresses) are made to recognise the errors of their philosophy of life.

At the end of the play Rhodophil and Palamede are jealous of each other and Doralice points the moral:

Dor. But you can neither of you be jealous of what you love not.

Rho. Faith, I am jealous, and this makes me partly suspect that I love you better than I thought.

Dor. Pish! A meer jealousie of honour.

Rho. Gad, I am afraid there's something else in't; for *Palamede* has wit, and if he loves you, there's something more in ye than I have found: some rich Mine, for ought I know, that I have not yet discovered.

[1] *Dryden's Major Plays* (1966), pp. 83–4.

Pal. 'Slife, what's this? Here's an argument for me to love *Melantha*; for he has lov'd her, and he has wit too, and, for ought I know, there may be a Mine; but if there be, I am resolv'd to dig for it.

The funniest character in the play is Melantha who combines a snobbish passion for royalty with an equal passion for everything French. She contrives to introduce at least one French word into every sentence and gets her maid to collect new words for her to use. It is a splendid acting part and as such was praised by Cibber:[1]

Melantha is as finished an impertinent as ever fluttered in a drawing-room, and seems to contain the most complete system of female foppery that could possibly be crowded into the tortured form of a fine lady. Her language, dress, motion, manners, soul and body, are in a continual hurry to be something more than is necessary or commendable.

Melantha has, indeed, been regarded as a forerunner of Millamant, whose faults 'serve but to make her more agreeable'. But Melantha's affectations are so exaggerated that she is more a figure of farce than of comedy and it is difficult to believe that men as intelligent as Palamede and Rhodophil should both fall in love with her.[2] It would have been more satisfactory, if less economical, to have kept her as the subject of satire and not to have made her one of the quartet of lovers.

Mr Limberham (Dryden claimed) was 'intended for an honest satire against our crying sin of *keeping*'. Because of opposition, the play was acted only thrice and Dryden removed those things which offended the audience. These could hardly have been indecencies— since so many remain—but were probably satire of individuals. Despite Dryden's statement of his intentions, there is some ambiguity about the results. Limberham himself is certainly satirised as a doting, deluded cuckold; and the amiable pander, Aldo, is also an object of good-humoured ridicule. But Eliot's spokesman,[3] who

[1] *Life*, chapter V.
[2] L. A. Beaurline and Fredson Bowers in their edition of *Four Comedies* of Dryden (1967) argue that because Dryden presents Melantha 'with so much self-awareness and unaffected candour', we 'cannot fail to be sympathetic' to her: 'Although we recognise her as the female fop, we infer some extra dimensions to her character, some inner spirit, a divided soul, driven by desire but conscious of her folly. It is the illusion of her inner dynamic that has contributed to this effect'.
[3] *Selected Essays* (1932), p. 45. 'The morality of our Restoration drama cannot be impugned. It assumes orthodox Christian morality, and laughs (in its comedy) at human nature for not living up to it'.

declares that the morality of the play is impeccable, seems to ignore
the hero of the play, the cheerfully promiscuous Woodall, who has
affairs with two of the women of the house, agrees with a third and
marries a fourth, the only chaste one of the four, without forfeiting
the sympathies of the audience. It is true that there is some attempt
to return to conventional morals in the final scene of the play:
Woodall's bride is determined to keep him faithful; Limberham
marries his mistress; Mrs Saintly has to make do with Woodall's
servant; and Brainsick is reconciled to his wife. But Woodall's
previous adventures are not morally condemned as they are treated
as amusing scrapes from which, with the help of others, he manages
to extricate himself.

But though the play is amoral, it need not therefore be condemned.
It obeys the laws of farce, not of comedy; and it should be judged by
appropriate standards. Characterisation is comparatively crude; the
dialogue is without any literary graces; but the action is rapid and
coherent and the situations extremely funny. When Woodall is
locked in a chest, or hidden in a closet, or embracing one of his
mistresses while the unsuspecting husband mounts guard outside,
we don't judge his conduct by any standards or morality—we
simply wonder how he will escape from his various predicaments.
The situations display Dryden's powers of theatrical invention, not
least when one of Woodall's mistresses lies under the bed which he
shares with another and the three of them are surprised by the third
pretender to his favours. *Mr Limberham* is a brilliant farce and, in
its way, a masterpiece.

The Spanish Friar (1681), has been praised by many of Dryden's
critics, including Scott and Johnson. The serious scenes contain
some fine verse and some good debate and a genuine tragic situation;
but the happy ending is forced, the psychology of the main character,
Torrismond, theatrical, and these scenes do not harmonise with the
farcical comedy of the underplot. Despite the title, the scenes
involving the Friar are subordinated to the others and their main
function is to exhibit the hypocrisy and greed of the Friar, and by
implication of ecclesiastics in general. Friar Dominic cheerfully acts
as Lorenzo's pimp while pretending all the time that his motives
are pure. Bruce King admits that Lorenzo and Elvira are lacking in
wit and gaiety but he argues that what he calls 'an unfortunate
crudeness in the sexual comedy'[1] was intentional because libertinism
'was going out of fashion' and because Dryden had 'developed a
new seriousness'. I can see little sign that Dryden was critical of
[1] op. cit., p. 160.

Lorenzo's licence or of Elvira's desire to cuckold her husband, who is depicted as a cowardly, impotent usurer. The revelation at the end that the lovers are brother and sister and that they had narrowly escaped committing incest is an additional bit of salaciousness. The satire of hypocrisy is funny in a crude way, but Dryden is appealing to vulgar prejudice.

The last of Dryden's comedies, *Amphitryon*, uses the plot which has been a favourite with dramatists from Plautus to Giraudoux. It falls outside the scope of this book because it is not concerned with the manners or morals of Dryden's own age, and is written mainly in verse. But it is worth pointing out that Jupiter, after seducing Alcmena in the guise of her husband, expresses the view of marriage which is found so often on the lips of Restoration gallants. He urges Alcmena:

> I love so nicely that I cannot bear
> To owe the Sweets of Love, which I have tasted
> To the submissive duty of a Wife.
> Tell me: and soothe my Passion e're I go,
> That in the kindest moments of the Night,
> When you gave up yourself to Love and me,
> You thought not of a Husband, but a Lover?

The name of husband is dull, he tells her; his tenderness

> Surpasses that of Husbands for their Wives.

When Alcmena tells him she gave him all a virtuous wife could give, he protests:

> No, no, that very name of Wife and Marriage
> Is Poyson to the dearest sweets of Love:
> To please my niceness you must separate
> The Lover from his Mortal Foe—the Husband.
> Give to the yawning Husband your cold Vertue;
> But all your vigorous Warmth, your melting Sighs,
> Your amorous Murmurs, be your Lover's part.

It is interesting to have Jupiter sharing the prejudices of the Restoration gentleman; but there is an underlying irony in that the real and the counterfeit Amphitryon, the husband and the lover, are indistinguishable to the virtuous Alcmena.

Dryden's achievement in comedy was uneven. Only one, *Marriage à la Mode*, is entirely successful as a whole; but *Mr. Limberham* is an excellent farce; and there are fine comic scenes in several of his other plays. His importance depends on the fact that he was the only real stylist before the advent of Congreve.

4

SHADWELL AND OTWAY

SHADWELL

'They say he puts no wit in his plays; but 'tis all one for that, they do the business'. (*A True Widow*)

Dryden's portraits of Thomas Shadwell in *MacFlecknoe* and as Og in *Absalom and Achitophel* have given him a kind of immortality, but not of the kind that any man would choose or, indeed, that he really deserves. As Saintsbury claimed, Shadwell 'had a much greater command of comic incident and situation' than Dryden and a 'much more direct power of dramatic observation of actual life' than Wycherley. What he lacked, and what ultimately has prevented the revival of his plays, was a gift of style. But, it might be argued, this very lack is what makes his dialogue a more faithful reflection of the conversation of his age than the epigrammatic brilliance of his greater contemporaries.

Bonamy Dobrée, admiring Dryden as he does, is not quite fair to his victim. Shadwell's plays, he tells us,[1] 'have almost every conceivable fault from the literary point of view'; they are 'the commonplace expression of a commonplace man'. Shadwell 'gave the outward appearance of a person, but never the idea behind, so that no knowledge of the human heart is added to us by a perusal of his plays'. But even Dobrée is constrained to admit that 'he has the great merit of reproducing the manners of his time'.

Shadwell was responsible for seventeen plays. Of these, *Timon of Athens* was an attempt to improve on Shakespeare, and *Psyche* and *The Miser* were an attempt, equally futile, to improve on Molière.

[1] *Restoration Comedy* (1924), pp. 117 ff.

Several of the remaining plays are of little account: but there are six or seven which show his talents to advantage. They include *The Sullen Lovers* (1668), *The Humorists* (1670), *Epsom Wells* (1672), *The Virtuoso* (1676), *A True Widow* (1679), *The Squire of Alsatia* (1688) and *Bury Fair* (1689).

Of all Restoration dramatists Shadwell was the one who kept most firmly to the Jonsonian tradition. He said he 'had rather be the author of one scene in [Jonson's] best Comedies than of any Play this age has produced', and he was particularly proud of the new examples of humours he introduced into his plays. He claimed, for example, in the preface to *The Virtuoso* that

Four of the Humours are entirely new; and (without vanity) I may say, I ne'er produced a Comedy, that had not some natural Humour in it not represented before, nor hope I ever shall.

In spite of the tone of this passage—and its absurd complacency is excelled in his preface to *The Miser* where he boasts that Molière's part of it 'has not suffered in my hands, nor did I ever know a French Comedy made use of by the worst of our poets that was not better'd by 'em'—Shadwell's theory of comedy is not despicable. He endeavoured in *The Virtuoso* at 'Humor, Wit, and Satyr'—to satirise, in particular, 'the Artificial folly of those, who are not Coxcombs by Nature, but with great Art and Industry make themselves so'. This is similar to Congreve's wish to depict characters

which should appear ridiculous not so much through a natural Folly (which is incorrigible, and therefore not proper for the Stage) as through an affected Wit; a Wit, which at the same time that it is affected, is also false.

Shadwell tells us again in *The Humorists* that his object had been 'to reprehend some of the Vices and Follies of the Age' and he dissociates himself from those writers whose ultimate end is to delight. His own aim is 'decently to please, that so he may instruct'—to create delightful images of virtue and ugly and detestable figures of vice and folly. His intention of

Conforming to the rules of Master Ben

may be seen throughout his work. Jonson, he declares in *The Sullen Lovers*, was 'the only person that appears to me to have made perfect representations of human life'. How closely he follows Jonson can be seen from the sketches he gives of his *Dramatis personae*:

Sir Positive At-all, a foolish knight, that pretends to understand everything in the world, and will suffer no man to understand anything in his company; so foolishly positive, that he will never be convinced of an error, though never so gross.

Lump, a methodical blockhead, as regular as a clock, and goes as true as a pendulum; one that knows what he shall do every day of his life by his almanac, where he sets down all his actions beforehand: a mortal enemy to wit.

The Sullen Lovers owes more to *Les Fâcheux* than one would suspect from Shadwell's preface, but despite his debts he contrived to make his play a satire of English manners. Stanford and Emilia are a male and female Alceste, disgusted with the insincerities and affectations of society, who are tricked into marriage by a gay couple, Lovel and Carolina. In Act I we are shown how Stanford is plagued by Ninny—a poet like Oronte in *Le Misanthrope*—Woodcock, 'a familiar loving coxcomb', and Sir Positive At-all. In Act II we see Emilia plagued by the same 'impertinents' and by Lady Vaine. Before the end of the play the two victims, after an initial suspicion of each other, are drawn together. There is very little plot, but the impertinents are neatly, if farcically, depicted; and the scenes of persecution are lively and amusing. Shadwell is equally good in showing us the reluctance with which the sullen lovers succumb to each other's charms, as when Stanford mutters 'Pox on her! how she pleases me!' or brings himself to a kind of proposal:

Stanf. The truth is, I think we cannot do better than to leave the world together; 'twill be very uncomfortable wandering in deserts for you alone.
Emil. If I should be so made as to join hands with you, 'twould not be so much an argument of kindness to you as love to myself, since at best I am forced to choose the least of two evils, either to be quite alone or to have ill company.
Lov. This will end in marriage, I see.
Emil. Oh, no! I dare not think of that! If he should grow troublesome then 'twould be out of my power to cast him off.
Stanf. Why, there's no necessity we should be such puppies as the rest of men and wives are, if we fall out, to live together and quarrel on.
Emil. The conditions of wedlock are the same to all.
Stanf. Whatsoever the public conditions are, our private ones shall be, if either grows a fop, the other shall have liberty to part.

The Virtuoso is one of Shadwell's most amusing plays but it is inevitably dated by the fact that the central character, Sir Nicholas Gimcrack, is designed to satirise the experimental science of members of the Royal Society. Most of the experiments he describes in the course of the play are closely paralleled in the *Transactions* of the Society, as Claude Lloyd has shown.[1] But Shadwell seems not to have realised the importance of the experiments of Boyle and others. He attacked Gimcrack partly for his absurd separation of theory and practice. He learns how to swim on a table and is horrified at the suggestion that he should swim in water. At the end, when his house is surrounded by a mob who accuse him of inventing an engine loom, he protests:

> I never invented anything of use in my life, as Gad shall mend me, not I . . . I never invented so much as an engine to pare cream cheese with. We virtuosos never find out anything of use, 'tis not our way.

Apart from Gimcrack, Shadwell depicts his normal quota of coxcombs: Sir Formal Trifle, who talks all the time in the style of Cicero; Sir Samuel Hearty, who dotes on amorous intrigues and disguises, despite his inevitable failures; and Snarl, a great declaimer against the vices of the age, who yet employs Mrs Figgup to whip him. The remaining butt for Shadwell's satire is Lady Gimcrack, who has a gigolo and contrives to seduce her two nieces' young men, but who talks continually of honour.

The incidents are mostly farcical. Trifle and Hearty are both deposited in a dark cellar by means of a trap door; and as Hearty is dressed as a woman Trifle attempts to seduce him. Funnier, and slightly more plausible, is the scene in which three guilty couples use the same hired room for their assignations: Snarl and his mistress, Lady Gimcrack and Hazard, Sir Nicholas and Mrs Flirt. As Snarl and Lady Gimcrack are both hypocrites and Hazard has shared the favours of Sir Nicholas's mistress as well as those of his wife, there are plenty of opportunities of comic confusion when the three couples meet. The young lovers are much less interesting. There are only two obstacles to their happiness—Lady Gimcrack's jealousy and the fact that each man falls in love with the girl who loves his friend—but the men agree to exchange mistresses without demur and the girls soon agree to forgive the men for having been seduced by their aunt.

[1] *Publications of the Modern Languages Association of America*, XLIV (1929), pp. 472–94.

A True Widow begins, like *The Sullen Lovers*, with a succession of coxcombs who embarrass the true wits, Bellamour, Stanmore and Carlos. These consist of Selfish, 'conceited of his beauty, wit and breeding', Young Maggot who 'runs mad after art, pretending much to love, and both in spite of nature' and Prig who talks of nothing but dogs, horses and sports. Bellamour and Carlos win the two virtuous ladies, Isabella and Theodosia. Gartrude, after being seduced by two men in a single night, is married off to Young Maggot. Old Maggot marries Lady Cheatly, too late to find she is poor. The main plot, depending on Lady Cheatly's method of cheating by the use of vanishing ink on legal documents and her Steward's attempt to blackmail her into marriage, is less interesting than some of the subsidiary incidents and characters—Lady Cheatly's brother, the puritan Lump, the foolish and amoral Gartrude, and, above all, Lady Busy, who tries to corrupt the young by her worldly advice. She tells Lady Cheatly that it would be a good thing to persuade Isabella to be a mistress of a wealthy man:

> Or, for aught we know, after he has tried her, he may like her so well as to own her—who knows? Be pleased to consider how marriage is cried down, and that there are few, that are good for anything, will think on't nowadays. Besides, custom alters all things mightily. Mothers very frequently do this for their daughters now.

Later on, she tells the virtuous Isabella:

> Now I say, since custom has so run down wedlock, what remains but that we should make use of the next thing to it?—good. Nay, not but that virtue is a rare thing—Heaven forbid I should detract from that—but, I say, the main is to be respected; a good deal of money— there's the point.

Lady Cheatly adds: 'My lady says right; 'tis nowadays more like marriage than marriage itself'.

In such remarks, or in Isabella's retort to Theodosia who tells her that Carlos has been reduced to offer her marriage—

> Then, it seems, he is weary of being your slave, and would make you his—

Shadwell shows that he could at times, though too seldom, be numbered among the wits.

The Squire of Alsatia is interesting for two main reasons: for the

picture it gives of the coney-catchers—the confidence-tricksters—of
the time and the extraordinary fraternity of rogues and vagabonds
who are able to defy the law in the confines of Alsatia (or White-
friars); and for the *exempla* it provides of two methods of education.
Sir William Belfond, a country gentleman, has two sons. The elder,
Tim, is brought up with great strictness in the country. He is chastised
for the slightest fault and is not given any opportunity of seeing the
world or of learning anything from books; nor is he given an
allowance. But, as his father claims,

> he knows a sample of any grain as well as e'er a fellow in the north:
> can handle a sheep or bullock as well as any one: knows his seasons
> of ploughing, sowing, harrowing, laying fallow: understands all sorts
> of manure: and ne'er a one that wears a head can wrong him in a
> bargain.

The other son is adopted by a kindly uncle who sends him to
Westminster School, the University, the Temple, and the continent,
'from which he returned a complete accomplished English gentleman'.
He is given a handsome allowance and is expected to sow some wild
oats before he marries. Indeed, the uncle cheerfully pays compen-
sation to his cast-off mistresses.

Shadwell, as one might expect, demonstrates that Sir William's
method is wrong. Believing his father to be abroad, Tim rushes up
to London and in a few hours is both debauched and swindled of
part of his estate. He acquires a whore and is about to be married
to another when he is saved in the nick of time by his brother.
Not that Ned is quite the 'complete, accomplished English gentleman' his uncle—and apparently Shadwell—believed. He is introduced
to us just after he has seduced the daughter of his father's lawyer,
he exhibits his education by approving of the setting of one of
Horace's odes—'Integer vitae scelerisque purus', apparently no
irony being intended by Shadwell—and, though he professes to be in
love 'even to marriage', he excuses the fact that he has just been
sleeping with a wench with the words: ''Tis dangerous to fast too
long for fear of losing an appetite quite'. To crown all, he is almost as
callous as Etherege's Dorimant with Mrs Termagant, his former
mistress, and the mother of his bastard, so that Truman his friend
asks him how he can be so cruel.

As it turns out, Ned is a good deal better than he seems. Mrs
Termagant is impossible; she has been treated better than she
deserves; and Ned's subsequent parting with the lawyer's daughter

shows that he had been unduly cynical about his relationship
with her.

The love-intrigue is perfunctory. We do not meet the two heroines
until the end of Act III and the only interesting thing about them is
the contrast between their appearance and their real characters.
They are compelled to act as pious churchwomen who hate the
pomps and vanities of this wicked world. But Ned and Truman,
who see them in church, realise that they are only pretending; and,
despite Mrs Termagant, there is no real obstacle to their marriages.

The play is swiftly-moving; there are some spirited scenes, and
the gradual realisation by Sir William, that his 'good' son is bad
and his 'bad' son good, is well-managed. It is, one imagines, one of
the two plays by Shadwell that could best bear revival.

The other is *Bury Fair*, written, like *The Squire of Alsatia*, at the
end of his life. It is not the only one of his plays set in the provinces,
but it is easily the best. Not very much is made of the fair itself,
which certainly does not dominate the play as Bartholemew Fair
does Jonson's, but Shadwell gives a lively satirical picture of a
provincial town with its *précieuses*, its fops, its wits, its boring horse-
play and coarse pleasantries, and its conviction that it can view with
the best of London society. We are made to see Bury through the
eyes of two fine gentlemen who in the end marry Philadelphia and
Gertrude, the daughters of Oldwit. For most of the play Philadelphia
has been disguised as Lord Bellamy's page—Shadwell was probably
imitating *Twelfth Night* as Wycherley had done before him—and
she does her best to persuade Bellamy that Gertrude is unworthy of
him. But this romantic plot, though better written than most of
Shadwell's, is of little consequence. Gertrude's ridicule of Wildish's
amorous rhetoric, though she really loves him, is in the main
tradition of Restoration comedy, and comes closer than anything
else in Shadwell's work to what Fujimura calls 'the comedy of wit'.

There are traces in the play of the moralising which a few years
later was to be the staple of sentimental comedy. Bellamy whom we
are meant to admire more than Wildish in the following passage,
has retired from the pleasures of London society at an early age:

Wild. Hey, my renegado countryman! thou hadst once the respect due
to good wine, fine women, music, wit and sense, and true pleasure.
Bell. For good wine, I could never be drunk but I did some mad thing or
other, which made me ashamed to show my face. For women, those
that were worth the having, were hard to come by, and harder to put
off: besides, the immorality of the matter gave me anxiety of mind;

> I saw men of wit, when they came to understanding, gave it over: and, when a thing must be done, 'tis best to do it quickly.
>
> *Wild.* Thou may'st as well say, since we must die, let's hang ourselves now: no, that's time enough, when we are weary of living. At your years, leave women and conversation!
>
> *Bell.* He that debauches private women is a knave, and injures others; and he that uses public ones, is a fool and hurts himself.

Saintsbury unkindly hints that Bellamy is a bit of a milksop and that Wildish 'is nearly, if not quite, the least offensive of the whole gang of Restoration comedy heroes'.[1] But this is hardly fair to Bellamy (of whose sentiments Saintsbury presumably approved) and, to most modern tastes, there are a number of Restoration comedy heroes who are more appealing than Wildish.

It is Wildish who persuades his French hairdresser to pose as a count so that the provincial francophiles, Lady Fantast and her daughter, may make themselves ridiculous by falling in love with him—not the best way of endearing oneself to the step-mother of the girl one hopes to marry. These scenes are admirable farce and there is some nice invective in the exchanges between Lady Fantast and her husband, Oldwit. But perhaps the best things in the play are the characters of Trim and Oldwit. Trim, based partly on Osric, using an absurdly affected style, convinced of his wit and breeding, and apparently effeminate, turns out to be not without courage and dignity; he is much more complex than most of Shadwell's humour characters.

Oldwit is even more interesting. We are not told his age, but as he claims to have known Fletcher and Jonson, he must presumably be nearly eighty. Shadwell, no doubt deliberately, makes his witticisms coarse and feeble, so that we condemn both the wit of the Bury *précieuses* and that of times past. But Oldwit is given Shallow-like reminiscences of his acquaintance with 'the great race before the flood'.

> I myself, simple as I stand here, was a wit in the last age: I was created Ben Jonson's son, in the Apollo. I knew Fletcher, my friend Fletcher, and his maid Joan. Well, I shall never forget him; I have supped with him at his house on the Bankside; he loved a fat loin of pork of all things in the world. And Joan his maid had her beer-glass of sack; and we all kissed her, i' faith, and were as merry as passed.
>
> *Wild.* This was enough to make any man a wit.
>
> *Oldw.* Pooh! this was nothing. I was a critic at Blackfriars; but at Cam-

[1] Mermaid, Ed., p. 349.

bridge, none so great as I with Jack Cleveland. But Tom Randolph and I were hand in glove: Tom was a brave fellow; the most natural poet!

From the plays we have examined, it will be clear that Shadwell had most of the qualities of a good comic writer. As Saintsbury claimed, he was, in some ways, a better comic dramatist than Dryden and he gave a more accurate picture of contemporary life than Wycherley. His characters, when he ceases to hunt around for new 'humours', are convincingly natural. But though he can be effectively farcical and even humorous (in the modern sense), his dialogue is lacking in polish, wit, individuality and style. This has been fatal to his reputation as a dramatist as most literary critics are more concerned with these qualities than with actability. Playgoers might well give a more favourable verdict.

OTWAY

Thomas Otway wrote ten plays between 1675 and 1683 when he died at the age of thirty-four. These included adaptations of Racine, Molière and Shakespeare, and two famous, if overrated, tragedies, *The Orphan* and *Venice Preserved*. His three comedies—*Friendship in Fashion* (1678), *The Soldier's Fortune* (1680) and *The Atheist* (1683)—have had few admirers. They were written during the interval between the masterpieces of Etherege and Wycherley and Congreve's first play, a period of some fifteen years during which little first-rate comedy appeared. Otway's comedies were apparently written against the grain. They have none of the talent displayed in his tragedies. Dr Ghosh, Otway's best editor, complains that his ribaldry is boring, feeble and unalluring; that his comedies were essentially fatuous, dull, empty, and purposeless; that 'their wit is of a poor quality', their plots derivative, and their characters uninteresting. Finally, Dr Ghosh applies to Otway's own plays a speech in *Friendship in Fashion*:

> And then their comedies nowadays are the filthiest things, full of bawdy and nauseous doings which they mistake for raillery and intrigue; besides they have no wit in 'em neither, for all their gentlemen and men of wit, as they style 'em, are either silly conceited coxcombs, or else rude ill-mannerly drunken fellows.

There is a good deal of truth in this indictment. Otway's heroes have little to recommend them except a certain coarse honesty; his dialogue is generally lacking in wit; his plots are farcical, but not funny enough to excuse their improbabilities, nor satirical enough to correct the manners of the age; and it seems sometimes that he is evolving his comedies from a study of those of his contemporaries.

His main theme is cuckoldry which he tries to justify by the behaviour of the husbands. Goodville, for example, the cuckold of *Friendship in Fashion*, plots to marry one of his mistresses to Valentine, and another to Truman; so that when Truman is seduced by Goodville's wife there is a certain poetic justice about it. Similarly, in *The Soldier's Fortune*, an attempt is made to excuse the cuckolding of Sir Davy Dunce by the fact that Beaugard loved Lady Dunce before her marriage and was campaigning overseas when her parents persuaded her to the match. Sir Davy moreover, is old, impotent, cowardly and stupid; he pays for Beaugard to be murdered; and when he thinks the murder has been committed, he accuses his neighbour, Sir Jolly Jumble.

But Otway apparently accepts without irony or reservations the current assumptions about marriage. In the first act of *The Atheist*, a sequel to *The Soldier's Fortune*, Beaugard tells his father:

> But sir, to make short of the matter, I am of the Religion of my country, hate persecution and penance, love conformity, which is going to church once a month, well enough; resolve to make this transitory life as pleasant and delightful as I can; and for some sober reasons best known to myself, resolve never to marry.

And when his old friend arrives from the country, where he has been enjoying the pleasures of matrimony, Beaugard remarks:

> Married! That is, thou callst a woman thou likest by the name of wife: wife and t'other thing begin with a letter. Thou liest with her when thy appetite calls thee, keepest the children thou begettest of her body; allowest her meat, drink, and garments, fit for her quality, and thy fortune; and when she grows heavy upon thy hands, what a pox, 'tis but a separate maintenance, kiss and part, and there is an end of the business.

His friend Courtine replies:

> Alas, Beaugard, thou art utterly mistaken; heaven knows it is quite on the contrary; for I am forced to call a woman I do not like by

the name of wife; and lie with her, for the most part with no appetite
at all; must keep the children that, for ought I know, any body else
may beget of her body; and for food and raiment, by her good will
she would have them both fresh three times a day; then for kiss and
part, I may kiss and kiss my heart out, but the devil a bit shall I ever
get rid of her.

Yet the marriage of Courtine and Sylvia at the end of *The Soldier's
Fortune* had been a love-match; it is depressing to find in the sequel
that the gay and independent Sylvia is reduced to a jealous, complaining wife. Otway makes little attempt to arouse any sympathy
for her—although there is one scene in which she is allowed to
plead with her husband in verse—and we are left with the impression
that this is just the way of the world. In the end Courtine catches his
wife in what seems to be a compromising position—the whole action
in the second half of the play is absurdly confused—and he is
delighted to have her in his power:

> Your humble servant my dearest! I am only glad of this fair oppor-
> tunity to be rid of you, my dearest: henceforth, my dearest, I shall
> drink my drink, my dearest, I shall whore, my dearest; and so long
> as I can pimp so handsomely for you, my dearest, I hope if ever we
> return into the country, you'll wink at a small fault now and then
> with the dairy-wench, or chamber-maid, my dearest.

How sadly Sylvia has dwindled into a wife can be seen by a
comparison with the following dialogue with Lady Dunce in the
earlier play:

Lady D. Die a maid, Sylvia? Fie for shame. What a scandalous resolution's that; five thousand pounds to your portion and leave it all to
hospitals, for the innocent recreation hereafter of leading apes in
hell? Fie, for shame.

Syl. Indeed such another charming animal as your consort, Sir David,
might do much with me; 'tis an unspeakable blessing to lie all night by
a horse-load of diseases; a beastly, unsavoury, old, groaning, grunting,
wheezing wretch, that smells of the grave he's going to already; from
such a curse and hair-cloth next my skin good heaven deliver me.

Lady D. Thou mistakest the use of a husband, Sylvia; They are not meant
for bedfellows; heretofore indeed 'twas a fulsome fashion, to lie o'
nights with a husband; but the world's improved and customs
altered.

Syl. Pray instruct then what the use of a husband is.

Lady D. Instead of a gentleman-usher, for a ceremonies sake, to be in

C

waiting on set days, and particular occasions; but the friend, cousin, is the jewel unvaluable.

Syl. But, Sir David, Madam, will be difficult to be so governed; I am mistaken, if his nature be not too jealous to be blinded.

Lady D. So much the better; of all, the jealous fool is easiest to be deceived.

This is quite effective in its way, but, of course, the sentiments expressed here have been more brilliantly expressed by later writers, Farquhar and Vanbrugh. This, indeed, is the trouble with Otway's comedies: we cannot help feeling that everything he does has been bettered by another dramatist. Only in the bitter comic relief in *Venice Preserved* do we have something genuinely his own.

There are a number of other comic writers who are superior to Otway. Aphra Behn, for example, though she never produced a masterpiece, maintained a respectable level of professional skill, both in plot, in characterisation and in dialogue. It is surprising that no attempt has been made to revive her work in the theatre, or to rehabilitate it in the study.

5

WILLIAM WYCHERLEY

William Wycherley was born before the outbreak of the Civil War and lived on into the reign of George I. In his youth he numbered Dryden among his friends, and in his old age his feeble verses were corrected by Pope. His four comedies were probably all written in his early thirties though, in his old age, he claimed that *Love in a Wood* had been written before he was twenty. Wycherley was not the first septuagenarian to become confused about his early life, but it is possible that his plays were drafted some time before they were performed. In any case the order of the plays is not disputed.

Wycherley has suffered more than any other dramatist of the period from the accusation that his plays are indecent and immoral. William Archer, for example, said that *The Country Wife* was 'the most bestial play in all literature'. Indecent his plays certainly are at times, but it cannot reasonably be maintained that they advocate immorality. In fact—with one exception which will be discussed later—his evil characters are satirised. Alderman Gripe is satirised in *Love in a Wood*, not because he is a puritan, but because he is a lecherous hypocrite; Addleplot in the same play is satirised as a coxcomb who is prepared to sell his mistress; Lady Flippant is ridiculed because of the contrast between her words and her deeds. In *The Gentleman Dancing-Master* characters are held up to ridicule for their aping of French and Spanish fashions. In *The Country Wife* the targets are the hypocrisy of women and the man who marries only because he could not keep a whore to himself. In *The Plain Dealer* Wycherley attacks the lechery and hypocrisy of Olivia, the treachery of Vernish, the absurdity of the litigious Widow Blackacre.

It is the sincere and faithful characters who are presented for our admiration, and it is marriage rather than extra-marital adventures which seems to be regarded as the proper aim. The faithful Christina is united to her Valentine; and his friend Ranger, after some ranging, is converted at the end, so that he objects to Lydia's ironical description of 'the insupportable bondage of matrimony'. Gerrard in *The Gentleman Dancing-Master* is prepared to marry Hippolita, even when he thinks her penniless. Even in *The Country Wife*, Harcourt and Alithea, whose object is honourable matrimony, are intended to enlist our sympathies in a way that Sparkish and Pinchwife are not. In *The Plain Dealer* we are invited to admire Eliza and Fidelia. So that Wycherley, if not exactly on the side of the angels, is not, as a dramatist, an advocate of sexual immorality.

Wycherley's first two comedies, however, are not primarily satirical. In *Love in a Wood; or St James's Park*—one scene of Act II and the whole of Act V are set in the Park—there are a number of interwoven plots. Alderman Gripe tries to obtain Lucy as his mistress; he is tricked into a compromising situation and agrees to pay blackmail to the girl; and at the end, as he is miserly, he marries her to recover his money. Sir Simon Addleplot and Dapperwit are rivals for the hand of Gripe's daughter, Martha, mainly for the sake of her fortune. The rivals are plotting against each other, and Addleplot is disguised as Gripe's clerk. Lady Flippant, Gripe's sister, rails against marriage but is desperately trying to catch a husband. In each of these intrigues the prize is shown to be of dubious value. Gripe discovers that Lucy is Dapperwit's cast mistress; Dapperwit discovers that Martha is six months pregnant by another man and that she will not inherit from her father; and Lady Flippant marries a man she does not love and who certainly does not love her.

The remaining plot—based on Calderón's *Mananas de abril y mayo*—is concerned with more sympathetic characters and has no direct connection with the other three. Ranger temporarily deserts his mistress, Lydia, when he meets Christina; and, though she gives Ranger no encouragement, Valentine believes her to be unfaithful. In the end, Ranger marries Lydia and Valentine marries Christina. The plot, which depends on the confusions arising from the wearing of masks, is typical of the comedy of the period, and so too is the conversation of Ranger and his friends. Dapperwit, who straddles the various plots, gives vent to a tedious string of similitudes when in company with Ranger and Vincent, like any other Restoration fop.[1] But the other three plots seem almost to belong to an earlier age: they remind one of the citizen comedies of Middleton. The gulling of Gripe is by a method which was often used by Elizabethan coney-catchers.

The success of the play is not due to the characteristics usually admired in Restoration comedy. It depends partly on the bustling action, partly on the amusing types depicted in it, and partly on its lively dialogue. There is some tolerably effective repartee, but very little wit. Dapperwit's similitudes are intended to be examples of false wit; but, like Witwood, he has one or two successes, and for the same reason—'he has some few scraps of other folk's wit'. His malicious coxcombry is well brought out in the first scene in which he appears (I.2). When Vincent is out of the room he slanders him to Ranger, and when Ranger goes out he slanders him to Vincent. He says that Vincent 'is obliged to the Bottle for all the wit and courage he has'. 'He has . . . no wit because he does not comprehend my thoughts'. Then to Vincent he declares that Ranger is false to his friends and a mere buffoon, without Vincent's courage and wit.

Vin. He has had courage to save you from many a beating, to my knowledge.
Dap. Come, come, I wish the man well, and, next to you, better than any man! and, I am sorry to say it, he had not courage to snuff a Candle with his fingers. When he is drunk, indeed, he dares get a Clap, or so—and swear at a Constable.
Vin. Detracting Fop! When did you see him desert his Friend?
Dap. You have a rough kind of a Raillery, Mr *Vincent*; but since you will have it, (though I love the man heartily, I say), he deserted me once in breaking of Windows, for fear of the Constable—

[1] It cannot be said that Wycherley made the mistake of allowing all his characters to be witty. In a letter to Congreve, Dennis (op. cit., p. 230) defended Wycherley from the charge, telling his correspondent that 'an express Vindication of Mr *Wycherley*'s ridiculous Characters, is an implicite one of some of your own'. He assumed, apparently wrongly, that Dryden was referring to Wycherley when he spoke of an author

who being too witty himself, could draw nothing but Wits in a certain Comedy of his: ev'n his Fools were infected with the Disease of their Author. They overflow'd with smart Repartees, and were only distinguish'd from the intended Wits by being call'd Coxcombs, tho' they did not deserve so scandalous a Name.

Dennis's defence is that the terms Fool and Wit are not incompatible or contradictory. People called wits may have smart sayings without 'one grain of Judgment or Discernment to distinguish Right from Wrong, or Truth from Falsehood.' Wycherley always avoided the mistake of 'making his Dramatick Persons speak out of their Characters'.

Dapperwit's detracting has, of course, the effect of raising Vincent and Ranger in our esteem.

The title and some incidents of Wycherley's next play were suggested by Calderón's *El Maestro de Danzar*. In that play Leonor's father, Don Diego, appears while she is speaking with her lover Don Enrique. She introduces him as her dancing-master. Don Diego stays to watch the lesson, but when Don Enrique confesses to Leonor that he knows nothing about dancing, she tells her father not to watch until she has had several lessons. When he persists, Don Enrique screws up the string of the guitar till it snaps. In a later scene Don Enrique quarrels with Leonor, and when her father arrives, she appeals to her lover to keep up the pretence of being a dancing-master. In Wycherley's play, Don Diego is the name assumed by Mr Formal, the hispanophile, and the Calderonian incidents are used in II.2 and IV.1. But apart from such minor differences as the substitution of fiddle for guitar, the atmosphere of Wycherley's scenes is totally different. They are laid in London, not Valencia. Don Diego is an eccentric English merchant, not an entirely conventional Spanish father, indistinguishable from thirty or more fathers in Calderón's comedies. Hippolita is a spirited fourteen-year old girl who dislikes the man her father has chosen to be her husband, the frenchified fop, M. de Paris; she extracts from M. de Paris the name of a witty, handsome man and, by an ingenious trick, persuades her betrothed that this man is his rival. M. de Paris thinks he is plotting with Hippolita to foil Gerrard, while all the time Hippolita is plotting with Gerrard to foil M. de Paris. She is hoodwinking her betrothed as well as her father.

Another difference between the two plays is the fact that Mrs Caution is present at the dancing-lessons in Wycherley's plays, and her suspicions are contrasted with Mr Formal's credulity. There is an amusing scene in the last act when Formal finds out that Gerrard is bogus:

Don. I tell you, Sister, he's no Dancing-master, I have found it out.
Mrs Caut. You found it out! marry come up, did I not tell you always he was no Dancing-master?
Don. You tell me! You silly Woman, what then? What of that?—you tell me! d'ye think I heeded what you told me? but I tell you I have found it out.
Mrs Caut. I say I found it out.
Don. I say 'tis false, Gossip, I found him out.
Mrs. Caut. I say I found him out first, say what you will.

Despite Wycherley's reputation, there is comparatively little bawdy in the play; and what little there is, is necessary to reveal Paris's character. In the first act both Gerrard and Martin reject the advances of two women of the town, Flounce and Flirt; but Paris goes off with them. In the last act they come to blackmail him but, when Gerrard steals his bride, Paris agrees to set up Flirt as his mistress. There is some admirable satire in the scene in which she lays down her terms—satire on fashionable marriage as well as on 'keeping'.

Flirt Nay, hold, Sir; two words to the Bargain; first, I have ne'er a Lawyer here to draw Articles and Settlements.
Monsieur How! is the World come to that? A man cannot keep a Wench without Articles and Settlements! Nay, then 'tis e'en as bad as Marriage, indeed, and there's no difference betwixt a Wife and a Wench.
Flirt Only in Cohabitation; for the first Article shall be against Cohabitation:—we Mistresses suffer no Cohabitation.
Monsieur Nor Wives neither now.
Flirt Then separate Maintenance, in case you shou'd take a Wife, or I a new Friend.
Monsieur How! that too! then you are every whit as bad as a Wife.

Flirt goes on to demand 'a large, sociable well-painted Coach', 'a couple of handsom, lusty, cleanly Footmen' of whom Paris must not be jealous, five hundred pounds pin-money, a thousand pounds a year present maintenance, and three hundred a year if they separate. Like Millamant, she lays down

that when you come to my house, you never presume to touch a Key, lift up a Latch, or thrust a Door, without knocking before hand.

But Millamant would not add: 'and that you ask no questions, if you see a stray Piece of Plate, Cabinet, or Looking-glass, in my house'.

Paris, with his passion for everything French, and Formal, with his passion for everything Spanish, are admirable caricatures; and the funniest scene in the play is when Formal insists that Paris shall follow Spanish fashions if he is to marry Hippolita.

But perhaps Wycherley's most surprising success is in the portrait of Hippolita, and in her love scenes with Gerrard. She is a convincing blend of the adolescent and the intriguing woman, ingenuous enough to reveal to her lover that she is an heiress, but ingenious enough to test Gerrard's love in a later scene by pretending that she is penniless. She is daring enough to invite a stranger to come and see her, and apprehensive enough to draw back when the time comes for her to elope. She is more than half the wooer, but her charm and innocence convert Gerrard from a Restoration gallant to a bashful lover, from one who expected only a sexual adventure to one who sought honourable marriage, even without a dowry.[1]

There are three plots in *The Country Wife*: one, to which the title refers, concerning the man who, for safety, marries an ignorant wife and is outwitted by her; the second, concerning the rivalry of a fop and a sensible man for the hand of the same woman; the third, concerned with the stratagem of spreading a rumour that he is a eunuch by which Horner secures sexual access to society women. The play is well constructed and the three plots are closely linked. The husband of the first plot is the brother of the woman of the second; and he is cuckolded by the pretended eunuch of the third. Apart from this structural economy, the plots, as we shall see, are linked thematically.

The Horner plot was presumably suggested by the *Eunuchus* of Terence; and, in view of Macaulay's complaint that 'the only thing original about Wycherley . . . was profligacy', it may be proper to recall Terence's plot. The hero of his play disguises himself as a eunuch in order to rape an innocent girl. Horner, however deplorable his morals, does not even have to persuade women to capitulate. Lady Fidget, Mrs Squeamish and Margery Pinchwife are anxious to surrender. But, of course, the audience is not required to condemn or approve of Horner's conduct. He is more a phallic symbol than a man. More precisely, he is a dramatic mechanism to expose the hypocrisy of society women—women for whom he has neither tenderness nor respect. His feelings for Margery are quite different. Macaulay calls their relationship 'a licentious intrigue of the lowest and least sentimental kind, between an impudent London rake and the idiot wife of a country squire.' Poor Margery is ignorant and unsophisticated, and not well versed in the way of the world; but to call her an idiot ignores the rapidity with which she learns and her cleverness in outwitting her husband.

Pinchwife, by any rational standard, deserves all he gets. It is apparent both from his words and his deeds that his conception of marriage is deplorable. His comment on Alithea's dowry is 'I must

[1] G. Weales (ed. cit., pp. xiv, xix) calls her 'a tease of the most unpleasant kind' and says that 'one wants to congratulate Monsieur on escaping marriage with her'.

give *Sparkish* tomorrow five thousand pounds to lye with my Sister'. And in the same scene he remarks that a wife who is 'silly and innocent, will not know the difference betwixt a Man of one and twenty and one of forty'.

> 'Tis my maxime, he's a Fool that marryes; but he's a greater that does not marry a Fool. What is wit in a Wife good for, but to make a Man a Cuckold?

Horner tells him that he did not expect marriage from such a whoremaster and asks him if 'keeping' is not better than marriage. Pinchwife's reply and Horner's comment on it are revealing:

Pinch. A Pox on't! the Jades wou'd jilt me, I cou'd never keep a Whore to myself.
Horn. So, then you only marry'd to keep a Whore to yourself. Well, but let me tell you, Women, as you say, are like Souldiers, made constant and loyal by good pay, rather than by Oaths and Covenants. Therefore, I'd advise my Friends to keep rather than marry.

In the next scene we see Pinchwife spying on his wife and the first words he addresses her are 'You're a Fool'. As Alithea points out, his attacks on the pleasures of the town serve only to arouse Margery's curiosity. He tells her not to

> be like the naughty Town women, who only hate their Husbands, and love every man else; love Plays, Visits, fine Coaches, fine Cloaths, Fidles, Balls, Treates, and so lead a wicked Town-life.

He locks her up when visitors arrive and prevents her from going for walks. He threatens to gouge out her eyes with a penknife and draws his sword on her both before and after she has been unfaithful. In fact he treats her brutally and stupidly, as a concubine rather than as a wife. When she outwits him, it is with the entire approval of the audience and his cuckolding merely exhibits the operations of poetic justice.

This plot owes a good deal to two of Molière's plays, *L'École des Femmes* and *L'École des Maris*. Arnolphe in the former play brings up Agnès in ignorance of the world, hoping thereby to ensure her fidelity when they are married. Such a plan is, of course, doomed to failure. Garrick's adaptation of Wycherley's play, entitled *The Country Girl*, reverts to the relationship of Arnolphe and Agnès, so that Margery can find a young husband and not commit adultery.

This was the version which was performed in London by the Lena Ashwell Players soon after World War I. The suburban playgoers were thereby spared some embarrassment, but Garrick's play is a dreadful adulteration of Wycherley's masterpiece. Even Molière's play, delightful as it is, is less plausible than Wycherley's and its satire strikes less keenly. But Wycherley's debt is unmistakable. The scene in which Pinchwife interrogates Margery about her meeting with Horner is clearly based on the corresponding scene in Molière's play.

Mrs Pinch. He kiss'd me an hundred times, and told me he fancied he kiss'd my fine sister, meaning me, you know, whom he said he lov'd with all his Soul, and bid me be sure to tell her so, and to desire her to be at her window, by eleven of the clock this morning, and he wou'd walk under it at that time.

Pinch. And he was as good as his word, very punctual; a pox reward him for't . . . But what, you stood very still when he kiss'd you?

Mrs Pinch. Yes, I warrant you; would you have had me discover myself?

Pinch. But you told me, he did some beastliness to you, as you call'd it; what was't?

Mrs Pinch. Why, he put—

Pinch. What?

Mrs Pinch. Why, he put the tip of his tongue between my lips, and so musl'd me—and I said, I'd bite it.

Pinch. An eternal canker seize it, for a dog!

Mrs Pinch. Nay, you need not be so angry with him neither, for to say truth, he has the sweetest breath I ever knew.

Pinch. The Devil! You were satisfied with it then, and wou'd do it again?

Mrs Pinch. Not unless he shou'd force me.

In the corresponding scene in *L'École des Femmes,* Arnolphe questions Agnès:

Arn. Outre tous ces discours, toutes ces gentillesses,
Ne vous faisoit-il point aussi quelques caresses?

Agn. Oh tant! Il me prenoit et les mains et les bras,
Et de me les baiser il n'étoit jamais las.

Arn. Ne vous a-t-il pris, Agnès, quelque autre chose?

[*La voyant interdite*]

Ouf!
Agn. Hé! il m'a . . .

Arn.   Quoi?

Agn.	Pris . . .
Arn.	Euh!
Agn.	Le . .
Arn.	Plâit-il?
Agn.	Je n'ose, Et vous vous fâcherez peut-être contre moi.
Arn.	Non.
Agn.	Si fait.
Arn.	Mon Dieu, non!
Agn.	Jurez donc votre foi.
Arn.	Ma foi, soit.
Agn.	Il m'a pris . . . Vous serez en colère.
Arn.	Non.
Agn.	Si.
Arn.	Non, non, non, non. Diantre, que de mystère! Qu'est-ce qui'il vous a pris?
Agn.	Il . . .
Arn.	[*à part*] Je souffre en damné.
Agn.	Il m'a pris le ruban que vous m'aviez donné.

In *L'École des Maris*, the other Molière play, Valère is brought a letter from Isabelle, which her betrothed, Sganarelle, believes is a letter from Valère to her and which she is returning opened; and Valère is brought to her lover, disguised as her sister, as Margery Pinchwife is brought to Horner. But, of course, Margery could not marry Horner, as Isabella marries Valère.

Mrs Zimbardo argues[1] that *The Country Wife* is based on Juvenal's Sixth Satire. There are certainly a number of resemblances. Pinchwife resembles Ursidius, the old rake who is driven at last to marry. The question of how far ignorance and rusticity guarantee chastity is discussed by Juvenal (ll.59–9) and so also is the behaviour of the rustic Thymele in the theatre (ll.63–6). Mrs Zimbardo also suggests that Wycherley substituted a pretended eunuch for Juvenal's homosexual and that there 'is a striking similarity between the scene in which Lady Fidget and her company of honourable

[1] *Wycherley's Drama* (1965), pp. 147ff.

ladies gather to drink and talk bawdy and the scene in Juvenal's
satire when women perform the rites of the *Bona Dea*'.[1] These
resemblances are probably not fortuitous, though Mrs Zimbardo,
perhaps, exaggerates their significance.

The possessiveness of Pinchwife and of the other husbands in the
play is contrasted with the foolish lack of jealousy displayed by
Sparkish. He is without jealousy partly because of his vanity, and
partly because he likes to show off his betrothed as one of his
possessions. When he is cheated of Alithea, he decides never to
marry 'because I will not disparage my parts'.

But, as we have seen, the main force of Wycherley's satire is
directed against female hypocrisy. Margery is comparatively sympathetic because she is transparently honest about her feelings; but her
naive truth-telling is presented as an absurd way of behaving in
society. Absurd, but endearing. The hypocrisy of Lady Fidget, Mrs
Dainty Fidget and Mrs Squeamish is anything but endearing.

Horner explains to the Quack the advantages of being thought a
eunuch:

> Ask but all the young Fellows of the Town if they do not lose more
> time, like Huntsmen, in starting the game, than in running it down.
> One knows not where to find 'em; who will, or will not. Women of
> Quality are so civil, you can hardly distinguish love from good
> breeding, and a Man is often mistaken: but now I can be sure, she
> that shows an aversion to me loves the sport, as those Women that
> are gone, whom I warrant to be right. And then the next thing is,
> your Women of Honour, as you call 'em, are only chary of their
> reputations, not their Persons; and 'tis scandal they wou'd avoid,
> not Men.

In the first scene in which we see the women on their own they
complain of the way men of quality 'never visit women of honour
and reputation as they used to do'.

Mrs Dain. Nay, they do satisfy their vanity upon us sometimes; and are
  kind to us in their report, tell all the World they lye with us.
Lady Fid. Damn'd Rascals, that we shou'd be only wrong'd by 'em! To
  report a Man has had a Person, when he has not had a Person, is the
  greatest wrong in the whole World that can be done to a person . . .
Mrs Dain. I suppose the crime against our honour is the same with a
  Man of quality as with another.
Lady Fid. How! no sure, the Man of quality is likest one's Husband and,
  therefore the fault shou'd be the less.

[1] op. cit., p. 150.

Mrs Dain. But then the pleasure shou'd be the less.
Lady Fid. Fye, fye, fye, for shame, Sister! whither shall we ramble? Be
    continent in your discourse, or I shall hate you.

Even with her sisters in iniquity, even after she has admitted her
own frailty, Lady Fidget pretends to be shocked and is continually
harping on her honour. Later in the same scene, when Horner reveals
the truth about himself, Lady Fidget uses the word 'honour' over
and over again, so that it becomes a synonym for dishonour:

> But, poor Gentleman, cou'd you be so generous, so truly a Man of
> honour, as for the sakes of us Women of honour, to cause your self
> to be reported no Man? . . . Well, that's spoken again like a Man of
> honour: all Men of honour desire to come to the test . . . But I have
> so strong a faith in your honour, dear, dear noble Sir, that I'd forfeit
> mine for yours, at any time, dear Sir.

In Act IV, Scene 3, when she comes to Horner's lodging for the
purpose of committing adultery, Lady Fidget again talks of her
honour, so that Horner exclaims:

> If you talk a word more of your Honour, you'll make me incapable
> to wrong it. To talk of Honour in the mysteries of Love, is like
> talking of Heaven, or the Deity, in an operation of Witchcraft, just
> when you are employing the Devil: it makes the charm impotent.

Lady Fid. Nay, fie! Let us not be smooty.

Only in the last scene—under the influence of wine—do the three
ladies drop their affectation of honour.

Horn. Han't I heard you all declaim against wild men?
Lady Fid. Yes; but for all that, we think wildness in a man as desireable
    a quality, as in a Duck or Rabbet: a tame man! foh!
Horn. I know not, but your Reputations frightned me as much as your
    faces invited me.
Lady Fid. Our Reputation! Lord, why should you not think, that we
    women make use of our Reputation as you men of yours, only to
    deceive the world with less suspicion? Our Virtue is like the State
    man's religion, the Quaker's Word, the Gamester's Oath, and the
    great Man's Honour; but to cheat those that trust us.
Mrs Squeam. And that Demureness, Coyness, and Modesty, that you
    see in our Faces in the Boxes at Plays, is as much a sign of a kind
    woman, as a Vizard-mask in the pit.

Mrs Dain. For I assure you, women are least mask'd when they have the Velvet Vizard on.
Lady Fid. You wou'd have found us modest women in our denyals only.
Mrs Squeam. Our bashfulness is only the reflection of the Men's.
Mrs Dain. We blush when they are shame fac'd.
Horn. I beg your pardon, Ladies, I was deceiv'd in you devilishly. But why that mighty pretence to Honour?

The whole of this scene is theatrically superb. The metaphorical unmasking of the women succeeds a literal unmasking and it is followed, first, by the realisation of the three women that they share Horner's secret and his favours, and then by the arrival of Sir Jasper, one of the cuckolded husbands, blissfully unconscious of his fate. Horner then has the difficulty of persuading Margery to return home and he complains that 'she betrays her Husband first to her Gallant, and then her Gallant to her Husband'. The country wife's natural affection is contrasted with the rake's ethos. With the arrival of Pinchwife and others, all is set for the denouement. Pinchwife tries to kill his wife and Horner and is only half convinced by the assurance—indignantly denied by Margery—that Horner is a eunuch.

There is no doubt that *The Country Wife* is Wycherley's most successful play. It was the most popular in his own day[1] and the only one of his plays to be frequently revived in the present century. Although some critics have preferred *The Plain Dealer*, the ordinary playgoer is surely right. *The Country Wife* is better constructed; the satire is more brilliant; and the scenes are brilliantly effective on the stage (e.g. Margery's letter and the *doubles entendres* of the china scene). The dialogue also reads well; but we never feel, as some critics feel with Congreve, that he reads better than he acts, or that we need to read it in order to extract the full flavour.

Anne Righter argued[2] that the trouble with the play is that although 'the centre of the comedy clearly lies with Alithea and Harcourt, Wycherley cannot really bring himself to believe in them'. Their marriage 'fulfils a symbolic role' but Wycherley's 'attention remains fixed' upon 'the man who flays romantic and social ideals'.

[1] Steele, *The Tatler*, No. 3, said that it was 'a good Representation of the Age in which that Comedy was written'. But, of course, Wycherley exaggerates for his satirical purposes.
[2] *Restoration Theatre*, Ed. Brown and Harris, p. 79. Mr Weales (op. cit., p. xix) goes further and speaks of Alithea as dull and stupid because she remains loyal to Sparkish for so long, and as corrupt 'in covering for Horner'. But she is protecting Margery, with whom she sympathises.

But it is not really necessary for the comic satirist to do more than hint at the standards by which he is judging aberrations and certainly unnecessary for the destructive agent to abide by 'the true wit's standard of natural elegance and decorum'.

The Plain Dealer was Wycherley's last play, written (at least in its present form) after *The Country Wife*. Its main source is *Le Misanthrope*, but Wycherley also borrowed one situation from *Twelfth Night* and perhaps the character of the litigious Widow Blackacre from Wilson's *The Cheats*, as Bonamy Dobrée argued, in opposition to Macaulay's conviction that Wycherley was plagiarising from *Les Plaideurs*. One scene is clearly derived from the *Critique de l'école des femmes*. But although Wycherley made use of these materials, the finished product is, as even Macaulay admitted, entirely characteristic of its author. 'It is curious to observe how everything that he touched, however pure and noble, took in an instant the colour of his own mind'. Viola, for example, disguised as Cesario, pleads Orsino's love with Olivia; and Olivia falls in love with the supposed boy. Fidelia Grey, disguised as a boy, has served in Captain Manly's ship, attracts the lust of Olivia, and is sent by Manly to the woman who has jilted him to act as his pimp. Olivia wishes to be Fidelia's mistress but not Manly's; and, at Manly's insistence, Fidelia agrees to an assignation, so that Manly can act as her substitute in the dark. Obviously in the world of *Twelfth Night*, the chaste Olivia would not propose sleeping with Cesario without benefit of clergy; Cesario would not agree to sleep with Olivia and would not cross the nice boundary which separates ambassador from pimp; and Orsino would not seek to avenge himself on Olivia by taking the place of another man in her bed. But Wycherley does make use of some incidents in Shakespeare's play, as when Manly suspects Fidelia of wooing for her own ends; or when he threatens to kill her to spite Olivia. Macaulay is hardly accurate when he describes Fidelia as a pander of the basest sort. She acts not for reward, but from love; she tries to cure Manly of his infatuation for Olivia and to dissuade him from his plan. A more legitimate criticism would be one of improbability. On the Elizabethan stage, when female parts were taken by men, it was easy for them to disguise themselves as men, and for the characters in the play to be deceived; but on the Restoration stage, where female parts were played by actresses, the deception was less plausible.

There are many resemblances between *The Plain Dealer* and *Le Misanthrope*. In both plays, the hero is one who loathes the insincerities of polite intercourse and who is in love with a coquette;

in both plays the hero is contrasted with a man of more flexible views (Philinte, Freeman); and in both plays two rival suitors of the coquette compare the letters they have received from her—in Wycherley the letters are identical. The introduction of the widow Blackacre may have been suggested by the fact that Alceste engages in an unsuccessful lawsuit. There are, moreover, a number of passages, which are virtually translated from Molière's play. The dialogue between Manly and Freeman in the first scene of *The Plain Dealer* is closely modelled on the first scene of *Le Misanthrope*; but, in place of Molière's examples of tactless truth-telling, Wycherley makes Manly tell the courtier he has a bad memory, tell the lawyer 'that he takes oftener fees to hold his tongue, than to speak', the man who has just bought a commission that he's a coward, and 'the holy lady, too, she lies with her chaplain'. The scandal-mongering scene (II.1) is likewise based on a similar scene in *Le Misanthrope* (II.4). Olivia accuses Manly of changing his opinion when it becomes another man's, because of his spirit of contradiction. In the same way Célimène says of Alceste:

> L'honneur de contredire a pour lui tant de charmes,
> Qui'il prend contre lui-même assez souvent les armes
> Et ses vrais sentiments sont combattus par lui,
> Aussitôt qu'il les voit dans la bouche d'autrui.

One other example may be given. In Act V, Scene 1, Eliza passes on to Olivia the criticisms made of her by others, as Célimène and Arsinoe do; but as Olivia is hypocritical as well as treacherous and lecherous, one of Célimène's darts is borrowed by Eliza:

> Elle fait des tableaux couvrir les nudités;
> Mais elle a de l'amour pour les réalités.

> That you deface the nudities of pictures, and little statues, only because they are not real.

But, despite such resemblances, and despite even a similarity of aim, Wycherley's play is totally unlike Molière's. This is partly the result, as we have seen, of the joining of the misanthrope plot with that of *Twelfth Night*, but even more of the difference of character and atmosphere. The fact that Manly is a sailor and has been away from London society, the perfidy of Olivia (instead of the mere coquetry of Célimène), and the betrayal of Manly by his bosom friend give him greater cause of misanthropy; but to Alceste's humourlessness and self-righteousness he adds self-delusion, boorishness and a perverted lust—for his seduction of the woman he hates and his demand that Fidelia should pimp for him can so be described.

It cannot really be maintained that Manly represents Wycherley's ideal. As Professor Lynch points out,[1] his conduct throughout the play

is not very far removed from that of a madman. He kicks his sailors and forces them to keep off visitors with drawn cutlasses; he cuffs on the ear a lawyer who tells him a lie; he takes by the nose an alderman who asks a favor of him; he threatens to cut his mistress' throat and his boy's too, if the boy will not hold the door while he wreaks vengeance on his mistress.

Mrs Zimbardo is equally emphatic that we should not identify Manly and his creator. To her his name suggests the 'natural man'; like other sailors in Restoration Society he is an outsider and a misfit; he becomes a hypocrite, disguising his lust,[2] 'a study in the corrosive effects of hypocrisy upon an individual soul', But although we may agree that Wycherley himself should not be confused either with Horner or Manly, there is evidence that his contemporaries believed that Wycherley was using Manly as his persona. Dryden called him 'manly Wycherley' and spoke of 'the Plain Dealer's manly rage'. The identification was natural. Manly satirised the morals of the age and Wycherley himself was a harsh satirist, more Juvenalian in *The Plain Dealer* than in *The Country Wife*; he was the author (as Dryden said) of 'one of the most bold, most general, and most useful satires, which has ever been presented on the English theatre'. It is doubtful whether Wycherley would have subscribed to all Mrs Zimbardo's strictures on Manly's character, for he is cured of his misanthropy and dismissed to happiness with Fidelia at the end of the play. Her faithfulness and admiration are surely a sign that Wycherley thought more highly of his hero than we can, or than he deserved.

Dr Righter is undoubtedly right when she argues that, by introducing Fidelia, Wycherley

created a genuine confusion in his own comedy. Fidelia is a character who must be accepted entirely uncritically, or not at all, like the heroines of Restoration tragedy. It is no good trying to regard her disguise and the situation in which it involves her as representing the education of a

[1] op. cit., p. 172. Mr Fujimura (op. cit., p. 146) similarly insists that 'the identification of the author with the vituperative Manly . . . represents . . . a total misunderstanding of the play'.
[2] op. cit., pp. 80 ff.

romantic. She is a fixed pole in the comedy, a character who remains unchanged from beginning to end. Moreover, she triumphs and, by involving Manly in her triumph, effectively negates all serious criticism of the plain-dealer and his attitudes. At the end, Fidelia's devotion restores the misanthrope's faith in human nature. Unlike Alceste, Manly marries at the end of the comedy. The trouble with this resolution, as Holland has pointed out, is that neither Manly nor Fidelia have really come to terms with the world as it is; their agreement is extra-social, romantic, artificial, and almost impossible to believe in. Even more important, it is the victory of excess.[1]

Whatever Wycherley's intentions, the reader is left uneasy at the end of the play. One says 'reader' rather than 'spectator' because there have been no professional performances of the play in recent years. This fact alone does not prove that it is inferior to *The Country Wife*, which is frequently revived; but, considering the reputation of the play and the praise it has received, it is surprising that producers do not give it a trial. But it would seem that the romantic and sentimental Fidelia is out of keeping with the rest of the play, that the Widow Blackacre plot is largely irrelevant, and that much of the play consists of talk rather than action, and when action does take place it is not at all credible. Of course, some of the talk is brilliant and it does throw light on Manly's hatred of society and Olivia's hypocrisy. The discussion of *The Country Wife*, though closely modelled on Molière's *Critique de l'école des femmes*, is even more devastating in its satirical impact, because it is used to expose the hypocrisy not of N. or M. but of a major character in the play.

Oliv. Very fine! Then you think a Woman modest, that sees the hideous *Countrey Wife* without blushing, or publishing her detestation of it? D'ye hear him, Cousin?
Eliza Yes; and am, I must confess, something of his opinion; and think, that as an over-conscious Fool at a Play, by endeavouring to show the Author's want of Wit, exposes his own to more censure: so may a Lady call her own modesty in question, by publickly cavilling with the Poets. For all those grimaces of honour and artificial modesty disparage a Woman's real Virtue,[2] as much as the use of white and red does the natural complexion: and you must use very, very little, if you wou'd have it thought your own.
Oliv. O hideous, Cousin! . . . but you are one of those who have the confidence to pardon the filthy Play.

[1] *Restoration Theatre*, p. 85. Holland, op. cit., p. 85, says that 'the presence of an ideal in a realistic situation signals the beginning of what we think of as an eighteenth-century sentimentalism'.
[2] cf. Molière, *La Critique de L'école des femmes*, scene 3.

Eliza Why, what is there of ill in't, say you?

Oliv. O fie! fie! fie! would you put me to the blush anew? call all the blood into my face again? But, to satisfy you then; first, the clandestine obscenity in the very name of *Horner*.

Eliza Truly, 'tis so hidden, I cannot find it out, I confess.

Oliv. O horrid! Does it not give you the rank conception or image of a Goat, a Town-bull, or a Satyr? nay, what is yet a filthier image than all the rest, that of an Eunuch?

Eliza What then? I can think of a Goat, a Bull, or a Satyr, without any hurt.

Oliv. Ay: but Cousin, one cannot stop there.

Eliza I can, Cousin.

Oliv. O no; for when you have the filthy creatures in your head once, the next thing you think, is what they do; as their defiling of honest Men's Beds and Couches, Rapes upon sleeping and waking Countrey Virgins under Hedges, and on Haycocks. Nay, farther—

Eliza Nay, no farther, Cousin. We have enough of your Comment on the Play, which will make me more ashamed than the Play it self.

Oliv. O, believe me, 'tis a filthy Play, and you may take my word for a filthy Play, as soon as anothers; but the filthiest thing in that Play, or any other Play, is—

Eliza Pray keep it to your self, if it be so.

Oliv. No, faith, you shall know it; I'm resolv'd to make you out of love with the Play. I say, the lewdest, filthiest thing is his *China*; nay I will never forgive the beastly author his *China*. He has quite taken away the reputation of poor *China* itself, and sully'd the most innocent and pretty Furniture of a Ladies Chamber; insomuch that I was fain to break all my defil'd Vessels. You see I have none left; nor you, I hope.

Brilliant as this dialogue is, it assumes that *The Country Wife* will be fresh in the minds of every member of the audience; and during the whole of the scene in which this critique appears, until the entrance of Manly, there is no action. All that we learn is that Olivia is a prude and a hypocrite.

Most critics, including even the hostile Macaulay, have praised the scenes in which the Widow Blackacre appears. Without the test of performance it is difficult to judge whether the character is as funny as it is reputed to be. It seems to be farcical rather than comic and not to blend with the comical satire of the rest of the play.

Of Wycherley's four plays, his first two are generally undervalued, and his last one, overvalued. But he is the author of one of the finest comedies of the period. Far from being immoral, he is at times overwhelmingly moralistic; and the triviality and dullness of which he is accused are two vices of which he can surely be acquitted.

6

THOMAS SOUTHERNE

Many readers have been puzzled by the lines in Dryden's epistle to Congreve about *The Double-Dealer*:

> In Him all Beauties of this Age we see,
> *Etherege* his Courtship, *Southern's* Purity,
> The Satyre, Wit, and Strength of Manly *Wycherly*.

It can readily be seen that Congreve combines some of the qualities of Etherege and Wycherley, but why Southerne? And why, in particular, Southerne's 'purity'?

Southerne is known, perhaps, as one of the writers who helped to prepare Congreve's first comedy for the stage, as the friend of Dryden, Pope and Swift, as the author of *The Fatal Marriage* (1694) and *Oroonoko* (1695). But only a few critics appear to have studied his comedies and very few have given them any great attention. They are dismissed with faint praise in the standard book on Southerne by John Wendell Dodds (1933).[1]

Born in 1660, Southerne outlived all his contemporaries, dying at the age of eighty-five: but the comedies with which this chapter is concerned were all written in the seventeenth century. He did indeed write one comedy, *Money the Mistress*, at the age of sixty-five, but this exhibits none of his real quality. His best plays were all written between 1690 and 1696 and the three good comedies at the beginning of this period—*Sir Anthony Love, or the Rambling Lady* (1690),

---

[1] There is a brief, but balanced, estimate in John Harrington Smith's *The Gay Couple in Restoration Comedy* (1948).

The Wives' Excuse; *or, Cuckolds Make Themselves* (1691) and *The Maid's Last Prayer, or Any Rather Than Fail* (1693).

The first of these, *Sir Anthony Love*, is outside the main stream of Restoration comedy. The scene is laid in Montpelier, not in London. But, except for an Abbé and a Pilgrim, the characters are mostly English in spirit, if not in name, as they are in the prose scenes of Dryden's *Marriage à la Mode*. Sir Anthony 'himself' is, in fact, a woman, and the main reason for the original success of the play was the attractiveness of Mrs Montford in the part, not merely because men in the audience were delighted to see, as the Epilogue has it.

The female *Montford* bare above the knee;

but because, as Southerne says in the epistle dedicatory, the best judges

never saw any part more masterly played: and as I made every line for her, she has mended every word for me; and by a gaiety and air, particular to her action, turned every thing into the genius of the character.

'Sir Anthony' is used by Southerne to satirise the behaviour of gallants of the period. She poses as a rake who is irresistibly attractive to women. But the motive of her masquerade is her love of Valentine. She has stolen £500 from her keeper, Sir Gentle Golding; and before the end of the play she has extorted more money from him, tricked him into marriage, and obtained a settlement of £500 a year by promising not to trouble him more. She does not attempt to marry Valentine. Instead she arranges for him to marry another woman because she knows that, since he is very much of his period, he is more likely to be constant with a mistress than with a wife:

I know you too well, to think of securing you that way . . . I know your engagements to *Floriante*: and you shall marry her. That will disengage you, I warrant you . . . *Floriante*, I grant you, would be a dangerous rival in a mistress . . . And you might linger out a long liking of her, to my uneasiness and your own; but matrimony, that's her security, is mine.

The play has some lively scenes, some good comic situations and some amusing dialogue. But it has serious weaknesses. It is not well constructed; many of the minor characters are uninteresting; and the humour is sometimes farcical, and not very funny. Very little happens in Act I and there is a great deal of talk about characters we have not had an opportunity of seeing.

Mr J. W. Dodds, in spite of a number of adverse comments[1]—'much that only seems like wit', 'the play is half again as long as it should be,' 'licentiousness', 'prurience'—regards *Sir Anthony Love* as Southerne's best comedy and it is the only one of his comedies discussed by G. Wilson Knight, who is attracted by the scene which to Mr Dodds is a blot on the play.[2] Sir Anthony makes such an attractive man that the Abbé tries to seduce her. When she reveals her sex, the Abbé, not being interested in women, hurriedly retreats. Mr Dodds calls this

an unsavory attempt of Southerne's to pander to the most depraved tastes of his audience

and he regards the dramatist's defence of the scene as specious. But there is no evidence that Southerne was appealing to homosexual tastes or, indeed, that he was interested in the bisexuality of which Wilson Knight speaks. The Abbé is depicted as a ludicrous hypocrite and the way in which he recoils from a woman is genuinely comic. Sir Anthony increases his confusion by pretending to be willing to be seduced:

tho' you know me now to be a woman, you need not keep a distance. What tho' I have disappointed you in your way, I may make amends in my own—

The scene, therefore, cannot seriously be regarded as a blot on the play; but the play is certainly less interesting than the others discussed in this chapter.

The main plot of *The Wives' Excuse* is concerned with the attempt by Lovemore to seduce Mrs Friendall. He has everything in his favour. He is young and handsome, and by the foolishness of her husband he is thrown into the company of the woman he desires. Mr Friendall is neglectful of his wife and unfaithful to her. In the first act, by a stratagem of Lovemore's, he is shown to be a coward as well, though public exposure is prevented by his wife's loyalty. With this knowledge, Lovemore makes two attempts on Mrs Friendall, but she repulses him on both occasions. At the end of the play, when Friendall is caught in another woman's arms, he is made to consent to a separation; so that Lovemore is not without hope that he will have better success with Mrs Friendall at some later date.

[1] *Thomas Southerne, Dramatist* (1933), pp. 63 ff.
[2] *The Golden Labyrinth* (1962), pp. 138–40.

The other plot is a complicated intrigue by which Friendall, thinking he is embracing Mrs Sightly, finds himself in the arms of a woman of dubious reputation.

The wives' excuse, as the subtitle makes clear, is that 'cuckolds make themselves'. The same point is made in the couplets at the end of the first act:

> Thus, who a married woman's love would win,
> Should with the husband's failings first begin;
> Make him but in the fault, and you shall find
> A good excuse will make most women kind.

Wellvile, who is to some extent the spokesman of the author, tells Friendall that he is writing a play, his account of it being a mirror-image of Southerne's own play:[1]

Well. You must know then, sir, I am scandaliz'd extremely to see the women upon the stage make cuckolds at that insatiable rate they do in all modern comedies; without any other reason from the poets, but, because a man is married he must be a cuckold: now, sir, I think, the women are most unconscionably injur'd by this general scandal upon their sex; therefore to do 'em what service I can in their vindication I design to write a play, and call it—

Mr Fri. Ay, what I beseech you? I love to know the name of a new play.

Well. The Wives' Excuse; or, Cuckolds make Themselves.

Mr Fri. A very pretty name, faith and troth; and very like to be popular among the women.

Wild. And true among the men.

Mr Fri. But what characters have you?

Well. What characters? why I design to shew a fine young woman marry'd to an impertinent, nonsensical, silly, intriguing, cowardly, good-for-nothing coxcomb.

Wild. [Aside] This blockhead does not know his own picture.

Mr Fri. Well, and how? She must make him a cuckold, I suppose.

Well. 'Twas that I was thinking on when you came to me.

Mr Fri. O, yes, you must make him a cuckold.

Wild. By all means a cuckold.

Mr Fri. For such a character, gentlemen, will vindicate a wife in any thing she can do to him. He must be a cuckold.

Well. I am satisfied he ought to be a cuckold; and indeed, if the lady would take my advice, she should make him a cuckold.

Mr Fri. She'll hear reason I warrant her.

---

[1] Act III, Sc. 1. The play has not been reprinted since 1774, so that an extended quotation is necessary.

Well. I have not yet determin'd how to dispose of her. But in regard to
the ladies, I believe I shall make her honest at last.

Mr Fri. I think the ladies ought to take it very ill of you if you do. . . .
Gad, I believe I can help you to a great many hints, that may be
serviceable to you.

Well. I design to make use of you; we, who write plays, must sometimes
be beholden to our friends.

Wellvile's last remark is, of course, ironical. He means that he is
using Friendall as a model for his cuckold.

It can be seen from this passage that Southerne's dialogue lacks
the exquisite polish of Congreve's, but it is often witty and pointed,
and nearly always appropriate to the speakers. What could be
better, for example, than this exchange in the first scene between
Mrs Witwoud and Springame? It brings out the feline hypocrisy
and corruption of the woman and the complete amorality of the
man[1]:

Wit. Methinks 'tis but good manners in *Mr Lovemore*, to be particular
to your sister, when her husband is so universal to the company.

Spring. Prithee leave her to her husband: she has satisfied her relations
enough in marrying this coxcomb; now let her satisfy herself, if she
pleased, with any body she likes better.

Wit. Fie, fie, there's no talking to you, you carry my meaning further than
I design'd.

Spring. Faith, I took it up but where you left it, very near the matter.

Wit. No, no, you grow scandalous; and I would not be thought to say a
scandalous thing of a friend.

Spring. Since my brother-in-law is to be a cuckold, as it must be mightily
my sister's fault if he be not, I think *Lovemore* as proper a fellow to
carry on so charitable a work, as she could ha' lit upon: and if he has
her consent to the business, she has mine, I assure you.

Wit. A very reasonable brother!

Spring. Would you be as reasonable a friend, and allow me as many
liberties as I do her?

A few lines later Springame is inviting Mrs Witwoud to his lodging;
but this is a little too casual, even for her:

Why, this is sudden indeed, upon so small an acquaintance: but 'tis
something too soon for you, and a little too late for me.

When Lovemore first pays his addresses to Mrs Friendall, she

[1] Act I, Sc. 1.

replies that her husband trusts her so completely that she cannot wrong him; but Friendall remonstrates with Lovemore for not complying with his wishes[1]:

> I desired you to sport off a little gallantry with my wife, to entertain and divert her from making her observations upon me, and thou dost nothing but play the critic upon her.

Lovemore asks how he should behave himself and Friendall fatuously replies:

> Why, I wou'd have you very frequent in your visits, and very obliging to my wife, now and then, to carry on our other pleasures the better; for the amusement, or so, you may say a civil thing to her, for every woman, you know, loves to have a civil thing said to her sometimes.

In Act IV Lovemore tries again:

> *Mrs Fri.* Well, what's the matter?
> *Love.* Every thing is matter of your praise, the subject of fresh wonder: your beauty made to tire the painter's art, your wit to strike the poet's envy dumb.

He has dropped inadvertently into blank verse and Mrs Friendall asks if he is turned poet. Then she continues:

> But to the purpose, sir; you pretend business with me, and have insinuated a great deal of pains all this day to get an occasion of speaking to me in private; which now, by Mr Friendall's assistance, you think you have ingeniously secur'd: why, sir, after all, I know no business between us that is to be carry'd on, by my being alone with you.
> *Love.* I'm sorry for that indeed, madam.

Mrs Friendall tells Lovemore that he might have known her better than to suppose his flattery could persuade her, and she asks:

> What have I done to deserve this? what encouragement have I given you?
> *Love.* A lover makes his hopes.
> *Mrs Fri.* Perhaps 'tis from the general encouragement of being a married woman, supported on your side by that honourable opinion of our sex, that because some women abuse their husbands, every woman

[1] Act I, Sc. 1.

may. I grant you indeed, the custom of *England* has been very
prevailing in that point; and I must own to you an ill husband is a
great provocation to a wife, when she has a mind to believe as ill of
him as she can.

Lovemore, who had proof of her husband's cowardice, and had
intended to put pressure on her by threatening to expose him,
realising that this blackmail will not succeed in its object, is compelled to regain Mrs Friendall's good opinion of him by handing
over the proof and pretending that this had been his intention all
along.

Lovemore makes one last attempt. The dialogue apparently
begins in the middle of a conversation[1]:

Love. Some can't get husbands, and others can't get rid of 'em.
Mrs Fri. Every woman carries her cross in this world: a husband happens
    to be mine, and I must bear it as well as I can.

She tells Lovemore:

I think you have proceeded like a man of experience in this business,
and taken the natural road to undermine most women. I must do
you this justice, that nothing has been wanting on your side.

She admits her husband's 'weaknesses'. She even admits that she is
not offended by Lovemore's attempts to seduce her:

Mr *Lovemore,* some women won't speak so plain, but I will own to
you, I can't think the worse of you for thinking well of me: nay, I
don't blame you for designing upon me, custom has fashion'd it
into the way of living among the men; and you may be i' th' right to
all the town: but let me be i' the' right too to my sex and to myself:
thus far may be excus'd: you've prov'd your passion, and my virtue
try'd; but all beyond that trial is my crime, and not to be forgiven;
therefore I entreat you, don't make it impossible to me for the
future to receive you as a friend: for I must own, I would secure you
always for my friend: nay more, I will confess my heart to you: if
I could make you mine—
Love. For ever yours.
Mrs Fri. But I am marry'd, only pity me—
                                            [*Goes from him.*]

This scene is remarkable in several ways. In the first place, it is

[1] Act V, Sc. 3.

rare in Restoration comedy for a wife to reject the advances of a
man to whom she is attracted. Secondly, it is rare for a dramatist to
deal with such a situation in such a cool and sensible way, without
righteous indignation on the part of the woman and without the
attempted use of force by the man. Thirdly, the woman's confession
that she finds the man attractive and his proposal a compliment is
psychologically truer than many of the reactions ascribed to virtuous
wives by dramatists of the period; and it is quite different in tone
from similar scenes written by writers of sentimental comedy.

Southerne, while writing for a society which accepted a double-
standard of sexual morality, is implicitly critical of it: Mrs Friendall's
refusal of Lovemore is set against the scene where Mr Friendall is
discovered in the arms of Mrs Witwoud.

One other point may be mentioned. The last eight lines of the
scene quoted above are in blank verse, though they are printed as
prose. Southerne, whose tragedies are all in verse, must have used it
in this case to heighten the rhetorical effect. Although Mr Dodds
does not mention the point, it may have been the unacknowledged
verse that led him to compare Mrs Friendall to the heroines of
sentimental comedy. But a play is hardly made sentimental by the
unexpected presence of a chaste woman.

It is clear from the dedication of the play to Thomas Warton that
Mrs Friendall's refusal of Lovemore was a disappointment to part
of the audience:

It is only the capacity and commendation of the common mistresses to
please everybody, to whom I will leave some of my critics, who were
affronted at Mrs *Friendall*: for those sparks, who were most offended with
her virtue in public, are the men that lose little by it, in private; and if all
the wives in town were of her mind, those mettled gentlemen would be
found to have the least to do, in making them otherwise.

Dryden, too, in his epistle to Southerne, also implies that the play
was comparatively unsuccessful:

May be thou hast not pleas'd the box and pit;
Yet those who blame the tale, commend thy wit;
So *Terence* plotted; but so *Terence* writ.
Like his thy thoughts are true, thy language clean,
Ev'n lewdness is made moral in thy scene.

The play, he tells us, was not damned or hissed,

> But with a kind civility dismiss'd.

He hints that the play reads better than it acted and advises Southerne to improve his plays by imitating the style of Etherege and the wit of Wycherley.

But Southerne's modern biographer, Mr Dodds, believes that the play deserved to fail:[1]

It is hard to understand how anyone could have expected [it] to succeed, even in 1691. A drearier round of cuckolding and wenching would be hard to find in any writer approaching Southerne in talent. Here is all the mechanism of the typical comedy of manners, with little of the comic spirit essential if the old comic skeletons were to be renewed in a successful dance.

He calls his chapter on the play 'a study in mediocrity', complaining of its indecency, coarseness, frankness and lewdness; but he praises the vitality of Mrs Teazall and the portrait of Mrs Friendall. Yet he says that, although this portrait is the 'most noteworthy thing in an undistinguished play', Mrs Friendall is akin to the sentimental heroines who followed her and 'strangely incongruous in her setting'.

These complaints are surely unreasonable. Southerne is criticised for using stock characters and stock situations of the comedy of manners and also for deviating from them in creating Mrs Friendall; he is criticised for coarseness and indecency, although his work is less indecent than Dryden's, Wycherley's, or even Congreve's; and he is criticised for being at his most successful in scenes of farcical horse-play, although, in his own age, it was thought that his plays were better to read than to see on the stage. We may suspect from the phrase 'even in 1691' that Mr Dodds had no great love for Restoration comedy; but readers of the quotations from *The Wives' Excuse* can judge whether or no Southerne rises above mediocrity.

Mr Dodds finds 'the same defects and the same thin virtues' in the third of Southerne's comedies, *The Maid's Last Prayer*. He complains of the lack of plot. Southerne, he declares[2]

balances three or four separate stories through a succession of scenes loosely constructed and throws them together at the end in a perfunctory conclusion.

[1] op. cit., p. 80.
[2] op. cit., p. 90.

He says that most of the scenes 'are congenitally dull' and that the characters are 'puppets who dance on [Southerne's] wires of sensuality or silliness'. Above all he complains of the nastiness of the characters, some of them being 'debased beyond most of their brethren in Restoration comedy'. In place of 'the verve and excitement of the chase', we get 'a coldly commercialised corruption'. But the oddest of Mr Dodds' complaints is that Southerne replaces the virtuous Mrs Friendall by the corrupt Lady Malepert so as to answer the public's demand. The complaint is odd because, as we have seen, Mr Dodds himself regarded Mrs Friendall as an incongruous figure in a Restoration comedy. Whatever Southerne does is wrong.

In some ways *The Maid's Last Prayer* is inferior to *The Wives' Excuse*. In the opening scene of the earlier play we are introduced to the main characters by means of gossip between servants. The exposition in the later play is less economical and it is more difficult to be sure of our bearings in the opening scenes. Then it may be objected that several of the plots are not fully developed. The one which gives the play its title, concerned with Lady Susan Malepert, who is described in the first scene as

> That youthful virgin of five and forty, with a swelling rump, bow legs, a shining face, and colly'd eye-brows,

and who accepts the hand of Sir Symphony at the end of the play after being disappointed of someone more to her taste, makes only brief appearances. Another minor plot is concerned with the relations of Mrs Siam and her husband, Captain Drydrubb. This plot, too, is rudimentary, though the Captain is a good acting part, and there is a nice final exchange when the couple agree to separate:

Capt. Why *Dolly, Dolly,* you should bear with the failings of your lord and master—
Siam. I do bear with your failings, you know I do, you old fumbling fool you.
Capt. And not betray the secrets of my dukedom, the mysteries of our bed and board, *Dolly.*

A third plot involves Lady Trickitt who, annoyed with Granger for refusing her money, passes on a note of his to Lady Susan, who takes her place, masked, at an assignation at Rosamond's Pond. Lady Trickitt, who watches the comedy of mistaken identity, gloats over Granger's discomfiture:

This is some sort of revenge upon the rogue for refusing me his money: how cou'd he imagine I wou'd allow him a favour, when he had given me such a reason to believe he did not think it worth paying for?

The main plot, however, and the most interesting one, is concerned with Gayman's love for Lady Malepert. He loves her but at the same time hates her because she allows herself to be sold to the highest bidder by Mrs Wishwell. In the dark, Gayman takes the place of the foolish Sir Ruff Rancounter. Lady Malepert falls in love with the lover she thinks is Sir Ruff and Gayman is torn between his physical infatuation and his hatred of her mercenary promiscuity. She loses in the end the only man she had ever loved—for, of course, in this respect her cuckolded husband is irrelevant.

The society bawd, Wishwell, is a brilliant portrait. It seems certain that Congreve, who contributed a song to Southerne's play, was influenced by one scene in which she appears. For in Act II, Scene 1, she is seen, like Lady Wishfort, at her toilet. But whereas Congreve's character wishes to repair the ravages of time by the use of cosmetics, Wishwell is impatient with her maid:

Wish. Pr'ythee leave fidling, 'tis well enough.
Christian Madam, you wou'd have your things sit handsomely.
Wish. Decently, I wou'd; what you call handsomely, is a niceness, wou'd as ill become me as a sultana does a fat body, or a high commode a lean face; and only serve to make my decays more remarkable.
Christian Will you please to use the wash—
Wish. I use the wash! a woman turn'd of fifty was ne'er design'd to be look'd upon: I may wash, and patch, and please myself; cheat my hopes with the daily expense of plaister and repairs; nobody will take the tenement off my hands.

There are some excellent things in *The Maid's Last Prayer,* but it is inferior as a whole to *The Wives' Excuse.* But both plays provide a devastating comment on the society of the day. Southerne, despite his 'purity', completely lacked Congreve's suavity. He lashes the crying age. Wycherley depicts a society of cuckolds and cuckold-makers, of promiscuity under a veil of hypocrisy, but the women, corrupt as they are, seek only sexual pleasure. In Southerne's plays, and particularly in *The Maid's Last Prayer*, the women are much more mercenary. One cheats at cards; another makes use of a bawd to obtain lovers for her, including some she detests; a third demands £500 as the price of her 'virtue'. The men, in their different ways, are as bad. It is quite wrong to regard Southerne as a dramatist who regaled his audience with bawdy for mercenary reasons. It may well be that the original audiences were put off by the uncompromising satire of his plays; and that he has not shared in the twentieth century revival of Restoration comedy because of his comparative purity.

7

WILLIAM CONGREVE

Congreve belonged to a Staffordshire family; through his mother he was descended from the Timothy Bright who invented an early system of shorthand and wrote a book which is thought to have influenced Shakespeare's conception of Hamlet—*A Treatise of Melancholy*; he was born at Bardsey, near Leeds; and, as his father was stationed in Ireland, he was educated at Kilkenny and Trinity College, Dublin. His first published work, the novel *Incognita* (1692), was written while Congreve was still in his 'teens. He was invited by Dryden to contribute a translation of the 11th Satire of Juvenal, and urged by the veteran poet to translate Homer. But when Congreve showed Dryden the manuscript of *The Old Batchelor*, he declared that it was the best first play he had ever seen. He and Southerne helped Congreve prepare the play for the stage and it was performed at Drury Lane in 1693 with a splendid cast which included Betterton, Mrs Bracegirdle, Mrs Mountfort and Mrs Barry. It was a great success and when it was published it appeared with laudatory epistles in which Congreve was hailed as Dryden's heir.

Southerne expressed the matter most plainly. Dryden was over sixty and the dramatists who might have been expected to succeed him had all faded out. Apart from Southerne's own there had been no promising comedies for twelve years.

> His eldest *Wicherly*, in wise Retreat,
> Thought it not worth his Quiet to be Great,
> Loose, wandring, *Etherege*, in wild Pleasures tost,
> And foreign Int'rests, to his Hopes long lost:
> Poor *Lee* and *Otway* dead! *Congreve* appears

The Darling, and last Comfort of his Years:
May'st thou live long in thy great Master's Smiles,
And growing under him, adorn these Isles:
But when—when part of him (be that but late)
His Body yielding must submit to Fate,
Leaving his deathless Works, and Thee behind,
(The natural Successor of his Mind)
Then may'st thou finish what he has begun:
Heir to his Merit, be in Fame his Son.
What thou has done, shews all is in thy Pow'r;
And to write better, only must write more.

In the same year, Swift addressed a verse epistle to the young
dramatist:

Thus I look down with mercy on the age,
By hopes my CONGREVE will reform the stage;
For never did poetic mine before
Produce a richer vein or cleaner ore;
The bullion stampt in your refining mind
Serves by retail to furnish half mankind.

Such praise might have turned the head of any young writer, but
Congreve in his epistle dedicatory speaks modestly of his work:

It is the first Offence I have committed in this kind, or indeed, in any
kind of Poetry, tho' not the first made publick; and, therefore, I hope will
the more easily be pardoned: But had it been Acted, when it was first
written [1689], more might have been said in its behalf; Ignorance of the
Town and Stage, would then have been Excuses in a young Writer, which
now, almost four Years Experience will scarce allow of. Yet I must declare
myself sensible of the good Nature of the Town, in receiving this Play so
kindly, with all its Faults, which I must own were, for the most part,
very industriously covered by the care of the Players; for, I think, scarce a
Character but receiv'd all the Advantage it would admit of, from the
justness of the Action.

Congreve confesses that 'if they who find some Faults in it, were as
intimate with it as I am, they would find a great many more'; but
he claims that to be aware of the faults 'is the first step to an
Amendment'.

In some ways *The Old Batchelor* deserved the enthusiastic eulogies
of Dryden and Southerne. Congreve had already acquired the art
of writing admirable stage dialogue, natural, easy, witty and appro-
D

priate to the speaker. Indeed, even in *Incognita* which, though a novel, reads like the scenario of a play, Congreve had displayed his mastery of dialogue:

Ah! Madam (reply'd *Aurelian*) you know every thing in the World but your own Perfections, and you only know not those, because 'tis the top of Perfection not to know them. How? (reply'd the Lady) I thought it had been the extremity of knowledge to know ones self. *Aurelian* had a little over-strain'd himself in that Complement, and I am of Opinion would have been puzzl'd to have brought himself off readily: but by good fortune the Musick came into the Room and gave him an opportunity to seem to decline an answer, because the company prepared to dance: he only told her he was too mean a Conquest for her wit who was already a Slave to the Charms of her Person. She thanked him for his Complement, and briskly told him she ought to have made him a return in praise of his wit, but she hoped he was a Man more happy than to be dissatisfy'd with any of his own Endowments; and if it were so, that he had not a just Opinion of himself, she knew herself incapable of saying any thing to beget one.

The narrative here provides only stage-directions for the witty repartees.

There are several scenes in *The Old Batchelor* which display the same mastery, and, in addition, with the power of differentiating character, as in the scene in which we are introduced to Araminta and Belinda:

Belin. Ay! Nay, Dear—prithee good, dear sweet Cousin no more. Oh Gad, I swear you'd make one sick to hear you.
Aram. Bless me! what have I said to move you thus?
Belin. Oh you have raved, talked idly, and all in Commendation of that filthy, awkward, two-leg'd Creature, Man—you don't know what you've said, your Fever has transported you.
Aram. If Love be the Fever which you mean, kind Heav'n avert the Cure: Let me have Oil to feed that Flame and never let it be extinct, 'till I my self am Ashes.
Belin. There was a Whine!—O Gad I hate your horrid Fancy—This Love is the Devil, and sure to be in Love is to be possess'd—'Tis in the Head, the Heart, the Blood, the—All over—O Gad you are quite spoil'd—I shall loath the sight of Mankind for your sake.
Aram. Fie, this is gross Affectation—a little of *Bellmour*'s Company would change the Scene.
Belin. Filthy Fellow!

Both the women in this passage of dialogue are characterised by the language they speak; and Belinda's affected speech, here and in other scenes, is one of Congreve's triumphs. She may owe something to Melantha in *Marriage à la Mode*[1], but she is a splendid creation in her own right. She is described before she appears as 'too proud, too inconstant, too affected and too witty, and too handsome for a wife'. Bellmour admits that 'she is excessively foppish and affected' and he pretends that he is mainly interested in her fortune. She mocks at Bellmour's 'poetical' wooing, and urges him to adore her in silence. In the last act she tells him, almost in the manner of Beatrice,

> O my Conscience, I cou'd find in my Heart to marry thee, purely to be rid of thee.—At least, thou art so troublesome a Lover, there's Hopes thou'lt make a more than ordinary quiet Husband.

She is afraid—and this is the explanation of her pretended scorn of men—that courtship is 'a very witty Prologue to a very dull Play' and that she will get from her husband 'only Remains, which have been I know not how many times warm'd for other Company, and at last serv'd up cold to the Wife'. This was a chord which was to be struck by all Congreve's later heroines, and Belinda, both in her affectation and in her charm, is a forerunner of Millamant. Congreve, even so early, contrives to give her a distinctive rhythm and turn of phrase, as when she quotes Cowley's 'Both the great Vulgar and the small' and adds: 'Oh Gad! I have a great Passion for *Cowley*—Don't you admire him? . . . Ah so fine! So extreamly fine! So everything in the World that I like'. Even finer—extremely fine—a passage that reveals Congreve as already a great writer of comic dialogue, is the speech she makes after she has been jolted to a jelly in a hackney-coach. Araminta tells her that her head is 'a little out of Order', and Belinda replies:

> A little! O frightful! What a furious Phyz I have! O most rueful! Ha, ha, ha: O Gad, I hope no-body will come this Way, 'till I have put my self a little in Repair—Ah! my Dear—I have seen such unhewn Creatures since—Ha, ha, ha, I can't for my Soul help thinking that I look just like one of 'em—Good Dear, pin this, and I'll tell you—Very well—So, thank you, my Dear—But as I was telling you—Pish, this is the untoward'st Lock—So, as I was telling you—How d'ye like me now? Hideous, ha? Frightful still? Or how? (IV.viii)

[1] See p. 51 above.

It has been suggested by Bonamy Dobrée that in *The Old Batchelor* Congreve 'chose Jonson for his master', both in his prose and in his method of characterisation. He is known to have been an admirer of Jonson, but it is difficult to tell whether the influence here was direct or through one of his numerous imitators after the Restoration. Several of the characters are mere types. Captain Bluffe, the braggart soldier, goes back to Bobadil and beyond. Bellmour might have appeared in almost any comedy of manners, though he is wittier than most. This does not mean that the audience is expected to approve of him: Congreve, replying to Collier, spoke of the character as a lewd debauchee. Sylvia has been compared to Mrs Loveit in *The Man of Mode*; but, as we are spared the scene of Vainlove's parting from her, she arouses less sympathy. Heartwell, the old bachelor, might almost have stepped out of a Wycherley play. He is a plain-dealer who falls in love against his will. He is ridiculed not merely by the men, who make him think he has married Vainlove's cast mistress, but by Araminta and Belinda, who appear elsewhere to be good-natured. The reason given for their brutal mockery, which we are told of incidentally, is that Heartwell had affronted Belinda's squirrel. The violence of Heartwell's feelings at the end of the play threatens to disturb the comic atmosphere. Herbert Davis suggests that this was to give scope to 'Betterton to move his audience by words of intensity and passion' but it may merely indicate that a born dramatist could not prevent one of his creatures from speaking according to his nature. 'Damn your pity', he says to Belinda:

> How have I deserv'd this of you? Any of ye? Sir, have I impair'd the Honour of your House, promis'd your Sister Marriage, and whor'd her? Wherein have I injured you? Did I bring a Physician to your Father when he lay expiring, and endeavour to prolong his life, and you One-and-twenty? Madam, have I had an opportunity with you and bauk'd it? Did you ever offer me the Favour and I refus'd it?

Vainlove, one of the two heroes, is the most successful of the male characters; and, if he owes something to Etherege's Dorimant, and perhaps to Townley in *The London Cuckolds*, he is not quite so egotistical, and he seems to be observed with greater detachment. His name is itself a criticism of his character, and Congreve was clearly alive to its absurdities. He has been so successful with women that he is sickened by his conquests. When Sharper tells him he has 'a sickly peevish Appetite', that he can 'only chew Love and cannot digest it', he replies:

> Yes, when I feed my self—But I hate to be cramm'd—By Heav'n there's not a Woman, will give a Man the Pleasure of a Chase: My Sport is always balkt or cut short—I stumble over the Game I would pursue—'Tis dull and unnatural to have a Hare run full in the Hounds Mouth: and would distaste the keenest Hunter.

This accounts for the way in which he hands over his conquests to Bellmour and for his callous treatment of Sylvia, who is regarded as unworthy even of Heartwell. The situation is not romanticised. Lucy remarks that Vainlove is 'the Head Pimp to Mr *Bellmour*'. It is only Araminta's refusal to capitulate that maintains Vainlove's interest in her. Sharper tells Heartwell: 'That's because he always sets out in foul Weather, loves to buffet with the Winds, meet the Tide, and fail in the Teeth of Opposition'. It is clear from the dialogue with Bellmour in III.iii that Vainlove wants the impossible:

Bell. Thou dost not know what thou would'st be at; whether thou would'st have her angry or pleas'd. Could'st thou be content to marry *Araminta*?
Vain. Could you be content to go to Heaven?
Bell. Hum, not immediately, in my Conscience not heartily! I'd do a little more good in my Generation first, in order to deserve it.
Vain. Nor I to marry *Araminta* till I merit her.
Bell. But how the Devil dost thou expect to get her if she never yield?
Vain. That's true; but I would—
Bell. Marry her without her Consent; thou'rt a Riddle beyond Woman.

Vainlove is a prisoner of the sexual conventions not merely of the drama but of the age. The conflict between the sexes in which both parties struggle for mastery, in which the conquered is despised, and in which the man therefore forfeits most of the satisfaction of victory, is exposed by Congreve and indirectly satirised. The crowning revelation of Vainlove's neurosis is his reception of the forged letter in which Araminta not merely forgives him for stealing a kiss but confesses her love. He tells Sharper that Araminta is lost—lost to him, because she has lost his love—that her love is 'an untimely fruit', and that he will snub her:

> 'Tis fit Men should be coy, when Women woo.

At the end of the play, when he formally proposes to Araminta, sacrificing his pride at last, she refuses to give a definite answer because, as Bellmour explains, 'she dares not consent for fear he shou'd recant'.

The only serious weakness in the play is one of structure. The Fondlewife scenes, amusing as they are, have little connection with the main plots of the play: they merely exemplify Bellmour's way of life and Vainlove's eccentric humour. Nearly three acts intervene between Bellmour's agreement to take Vainlove's place at the assignation and his carrying the plan into execution. Although this is a means of emphasising the unity of time, it is, from the audience's point of view, too long a gap.

Congreve's next play, *The Double Dealer*, was produced in the following year; and, when it was published, it appeared with Dryden's famous epistle:

> Well then; the promis'd hour is come at last;
> The present Age of Wit obscures the past.

Congreve is saluted as the superior of Jonson and Fletcher and as combining the merits of contemporary dramatists:

> In Him all Beauties of this Age we see,
> *Etherege* his Courtship, *Southern*'s Purity;
> The Satire, Wit, and Strength of Manly *Witcherly*.

He was even the equal of Shakespeare:

> Heav'n that but once was Prodigal before,
> To *Shakespeare* gave as much; she cou'd not give him more.

And, in the last lines, Congreve, 'whom ev'ry Muse and Grace adorn', is implored to defend, even against his judgement, his 'departed Friend', Dryden. Even when due allowance has been made for the hyperboles of congratulatory epistles, Dryden's praise is sufficiently remarkable and it contrasts with the fate of the play both on its first performance and later. Dryden told Walsh that 'it was much censured by the greater part of the Town; and is defended onely by the best Judges, who, as you know, are commonly the fewest'.

Congreve was jolted from his customary modest serenity by his consciousness that the play was greatly superior to the one everybody had praised. His epistle dedicatory contains an attack on his 'illiterate critics' and the 'Ignorance and Malice of the greater part of his Audience'. He had tried to write 'a true and regular Comedy' and, he claimed, the Mechanical part of it is perfect. That, I may say with as little vanity, as a Builder may say he has built a House according to the Model laid down before him; or a Gardiner that he has set his Flowers in a knot of such or such a Figure. I design'd the Moral first, and to that Moral I invented the Fable, and do not know that I have borrow'd one hint of it any where. I made the Plot as strong as I could, because it was single, and I made it single, because I would avoid confusion and was resolved to preserve the three Unities of the Drama, which I have visibly done to the utmost severity.

Congreve might have added that the characters are well-drawn and that the dialogue is more continuously brilliant than that of any previous comedy of manners. The relative unpopularity of the play may be due to the feeling that the Iago-like villainy of Maskwell[1] and the violent passions of Lady Touchwood (in love with her nephew) blend rather awkwardly with the satirical comedy of the Froths and the Plyants. This is a feeling that has been expressed by more recent critics. The original audience may also have been annoyed by the unflattering picture Congreve presented of society.[2] We know from the epistle dedicatory that some women were offended because he had represented some of their sex as vicious and affected. 'How can I help it?' Congreve asked:

It is the Business of a Comick Poet to paint the Vices and Follies of Human kind; and there are but two sexes that I know, *viz. Men* and *Women*, which have a Title to Humanity: And if I leave one half of them out, the Work will be imperfect.

In his assumption that the function of comedy was to correct the manners or morals of society, Congreve, as he claimed in his reply to Collier, was following classical precedent:

Comedy (says *Aristotle*) is an Imitation of the worse sort of People . . . He does not mean the worse sort of People in respect to their Quality, but in respect to their Manners . . . The Vices most frequent, and which are the common Practice of the looser sort of Livers, are the subject Matter of Comedy. He tells us farther, that they must be exposed after a ridiculous manner: For Men are to be laugh'd out of their Vices in Comedy; the

[1] That Congreve was thinking of Iago may be deduced from his use of the phrase 'ocular proof'.
[2] Dryden told Walsh that 'the women think he has exposed their Bitchery too much; & the Gentlemen are offended with him for the discovery of their follyes; & the way of their Intrigues, under the notion of Friendship to their Ladyes Husbands'.

Business of Comedy is to delight as well as to instruct: And as vicious People are made ashamed of their Follies or Faults, by seeing them exposed in a ridiculous manner, so are good People at once both warned and diverted at their Expence.[1]

In *The Double Dealer*, Congreve was not polishing vices so that they seemed like perfections (as was said of Etherege); he was displaying them in a harsh, satirical light.

Another objection to the play—Maskwell's soliloquies—Congreve attempts to answer. What he says on the matter is sensible enough:

We ought not to imagine that this Man either talks to us, or to himself; he is only thinking, and thinking such Matter as were inexcusable Folly in him to speak.

With a Maskwell or an Iago soliloquy is a necessary means of informing the audience of the character's villainy. But Congreve evades the real objection to one of the soliloquies in the play. In spite of his admission that if a man 'suppose any one to be by, when he talks to himself, it is monstrous and ridiculous to the last degree', he allows Maskwell at the beginning of Act V to talk to himself of his love for Cynthia, so that he will be overheard by Lord Touchwood.

A final objection to the play is the improbability of Maskwell's plot to marry Cynthia while she believes she is marrying Mellefont. A similar device in *The Old Batchelor*, when Sir Joseph Wittol marries Sylvia in mistake for Araminta, and one in *Love for Love*, where Tattle, meaning to marry Angelica, finds himself married to Mrs Frail, who thought she was marrying Valentine, are both in a different category because less plausibility is demanded in a farcical context.

On one point, Congreve's defence is sound. People complained that the hero is a gull. To this Congreve replied:

Is every Man a Gull and a Fool that is deceiv'd? At that rate I'm afraid the two Classes of Men will be reduc'd to one, and the Knaves themselves be at a loss to justifie their Title: But if an Open-hearted honest Man, who has an entire Confidence in one whom he takes to be his Friend, and whom he has oblig'd to be so; and who (to confirm him in his Opinion) in all Appearance, and upon several Trials has been so: If this Man be deceiv'd by the Treachery of the other: must he of necessity commence Fool immediately, only because the other has prov'd a Villain?

[1] Ed. Dobrée, p. 408.

The play, however, is not as seriously damaged by these faults as its reception would suggest. The plot is exciting. The schemes of Mellefont to foil his aunt, and the counter-scheme of Lady Touchwood and Maskwell, keep the audience in suspense until the last few minutes of the play. In Lady Touchwood's incestuous passion for Mellefont and her determination to be revenged on him for rejecting her advances, we are almost in the same world as Racine's tragedies.[1] Lady Touchwood wishes first to disinherit Mellefont by bearing Maskwell's child, then to prevent his marriage to Cynthia by accusing him of attempted rape, and finally to ruin him after blackmailing him into complying with her desires. Yet she is right in thinking that her violent passions have more excuse than the cold-blooded lechery and treachery of Maskwell, 'a sedate, a thinking Villain, whose black Blood runs temperately bad'.

The comic scenes are carefully dovetailed into the serious intrigue. Lady Plyant's willingness to be seduced by Mellefont is a comic parallel to Lady Touchwood's incestuous desires, and her actual seduction by Careless is a by-product of Mellefont's scheme to win her to his side. 'She's handsome, and knows it; is very silly, and thinks she has Sense, and has an old fond Husband'. Sir Paul, indeed, dotes upon her so much that he is completely enslaved, though seldom or never allowed to touch her. The Froths are fools of another kind. Lord Froth, the solemn coxcomb thinks it beneath his dignity to laugh:[2]

Sir Paul And, my Lord *Froth*, your Lordship is so merry a Man, he, he, he.

Lord Froth O foy, Sir *Paul*, what do you mean? Merry! O Barbarous! I'd as lieve you call'd me a Fool.

Sir Paul Nay I protest and vow now, 'tis true; when Mr *Brisk* Jokes, your Lordship's Laugh does so become you, he, he, he.

Lord Froth Ridiculous . . . I assure you, Sir *Paul*, I laugh at no bodies Jest but my own, or a Lady's; I assure you, Sir *Paul*.

Brisk How? how, my Lord? What, affront my Wit! Let me perish, do I never say anything worthy to be Laughed at?

Lord Froth O foy, don't misapprehend me, I don't say so, for I often smile at your Conceptions. But there is nothing more unbecoming a Man of Quality, than to Laugh; Jesu, 'tis such a vulgar expression of the Passion! every body can Laugh. Then especially to Laugh at the

[1] Even the prose sometimes seems to be in danger of turning into verse; but Congreve, unlike his contemporaries, never quite falls into the trap.
[2] This is one of Congreve's rare debts to Molière. cf. *La Critique de l'école des Femmes*, scene 5.

D*

Jest of an Inferior Person, or when any body else of the same Quality
does not Laugh with him. Ridiculous! To be pleased with what
pleases the Croud! Now when I Laugh, I always Laugh alone.
Brisk I suppose that's because you Laugh at your own Jests.

*   *   *   *

Mellefont But does your Lordship never see Comedies.
Lord Froth O yes, sometimes—but I never Laugh.
Mellefont No?
Lord Froth Oh, no.—Never Laugh indeed, Sir.
Careless No, why what d'ee go there for?
Lord Froth To distinguish myself from the Commonalty, and mortify
the Poets . . . I swear,—he, he, he, I have often constrained my Incli-
nations to Laugh—He, he, he, to avoid giving them encouragement.

Lady Froth is equally silly. She is 'a pretender to Poetry, Wit and
Learning', writes inane verses, and is easily seduced by the 'pert
coxcomb', Brisk:

Brisk The Deuce take me, I can't help laughing my self neither, ha ha ha;
yet by Heavens I have a violent Passion for your Ladiship, seriously.
Lady Froth Seriously? Ha ha ha.
Brisk Seriously, ha ha ha. Gad I have, for all I Laugh.
Lady Froth Ha ha ha! What d'ye think I Laugh at? Ha ha ha.
Brisk Me I'gad, ha ha.
Lady Froth No the Deuce take me if I don't Laugh at my self; for hang
me if I have not a violent Passion for Mr *Brisk*, ha ha ha.

It is the absurdities of the Froths and the Plyants that make
Cynthia hesitate about marriage: all through the play her sense and
sensibility are contrasted with the aberrations of the other women;
and she is given a soliloquy, significantly placed at the end of an
act, which enables Congreve to comment through her mouth:

'Tis not so hard to counterfeit Joy in the depth of Affliction, as to
dissemble Mirth in Company of Fools—Why should I call 'em Fools?
The World thinks better of 'em; for these have Quality and Education,
Wit and fine Conversation, are receiv'd and admir'd by the World
—If not, they like and admire themselves—And why is not that true
Wisdom, for 'tis Happiness: And for ought I know, we have mis-
apply'd the Name all this while, and mistaken the thing: Since
If Happiness in Self-Content is plac'd,
The Wise are Wretched, and Fools only Bless'd.

Congreve tells his readers in the epistle dedicatory that 'It is the Business of a Comick Poet to paint the Vices and Follies of Human-kind'; and in his answer to Jeremy Collier (who had attacked *The Double Dealer*) he made the same point. He therefore lashed the follies of Sir Paul and Lord Froth, the folly and immorality of their wives, the ungovernable passions of Lady Touchwood, the credulity of her husband, and the hypocrisy and wickedness of Maskwell: but, as in all his comedies, he depicts also a pair of lovers who (at least in comparison with the circle in which they move) deserve their happiness.

In *Love for Love* Congreve follows the same pattern, except that he excludes examples of monstrous wickedness and concentrates on the follies and sexual irregularities of his characters—the super-stition of Foresight, the adultery of his wife, the simplicity of Miss Prue, the frailty of Mrs Frail, the vanity of Tattle, the egotism and arbitrariness of Sir Sampson Legend, the satirical humour of Scandal. Ben is used, much as Sir Wilfull Witwoud was later to be used, partly as a means of showing up the artificiality of society and partly as the target for good-natured satire on his uncouth ways and nautical vocabulary. Valentine himself has been a rake: he is about to be disinherited by his father for his extravagant way of life, and he has at least one bastard. He has therefore to undergo proba-tion and prove to Angelica that he is constant in his love and not merely anxious to secure her fortune. In view of the alleged artifi-ciality of Congreve's comedies, it may be as well to stress the unromantic way in which he deals with questions of money. Four of his heroines have fortunes the heroes do not wish to forfeit; and the protection of Mrs Fainall's fortune from her husband is the climax of *The Way of the World*. The motto from Horace on the title-page of that play was not chosen at random: '*Metuat doti deprensa*'.[1]

Valentine's feigned madness enabled Congreve to extend the

---

[1] W. W. Appleton, in *Beaumont and Fletcher* (1956), pp. 91–2, has suggested that the title and some details of *Love for Love* were derived from *The Elder Brother*. Charles, in that play, asks the heroine 'Can you love for love, and make that the reward?' The heroine's name is Angellina, not unlike Congreve's Angelica; and Brisac's attempt to persuade his elder son to sign away his inheritance to his brother has some resemblance to Sir Sampson's attempt to make Valentine sign away his inheritance to Ben. But, on the other hand, there would seem to be no evidence to support Appleton's contention that Congreve was influenced by the proposal scene or by Fletcher's prose in that play. The whole play was printed as prose in Second Folio but in the quarto it is properly printed as verse with not a single line of prose.

range of his satire to cover the law, trade, religion, the court, friendship and woman. It outraged Collier that Valentine should say, more than once, 'I am Truth'; but, of course, no blasphemy was intended. It was merely a way of emphasising the essential seriousness of the madman's criticisms of society. Like the mad Lear, or the sage Fool, or Poor Tom, Valentine mixes 'matter and impertinency'. The mad scenes also freed Congreve from the restraints of realism, so that he could use a more poetical style than he had allowed himself in his previous comedies—more truly poetical, indeed, than anything in *The Mourning Bride* or his other writings in verse. But it should be noted that Congreve is careful to temper his most haunting passages with wit so that we are never in danger of being cloyed by them:

Tattle Do you know me, *Valentine*?
Valentine You? Who are you? No, I hope not.
Tattle I am *Jack Tattle*, your Friend.
Valentine My Friend, what to do? I am no Married Man, and thou can'st not lie with my Wife? I am very poor, and thou can'st not borrow Money of me; Then what Employment have I for a Friend.
Tattle Hah! A good open Speaker, and not to be trusted with a Secret.
Angelica Do you know me, *Valentine*?
Valentine Oh very well.
Angelica Who am I?
Valentine You're a Woman,—One to whom Heav'n gave Beauty, when it grafted Roses on a Briar. You are the reflection of Heav'n in a Pond, and he that leaps at you is sunk. You are all white, a sheet of lovely spotless Paper, when you first are Born; but you are to be scrawl'd and blotted by every Goose's Quill. I know you; for I lov'd a Woman, and lov'd her so long, that I found out a strange thing: I found out what a Woman was good for.
Tattle Aye, prithee, what's that?
Valentine Why to keep a Secret.
Tattle O Lord!
Valentine O exceeding good to keep a Secret: For tho' she should tell, yet she is not to be believ'd.

The passage needs to be read in its context for its full flavour to be appreciated. It is necessary to know that, as Valentine is pretending to take Mrs Frail for Angelica, he must also pretend not to recognise Angelica when she visits him; that Angelica has told Tattle not to tell anyone that she loves Valentine, expecting him to do the opposite, since he cannot keep a secret; and that Tattle has just betrayed Valentine by making advances to Angelica. The exquisite cadences of

Valentine's longest speech are framed by cutting remarks about false friendship and the inability of women to keep a secret—and this last has been suggested by Tattle's remark a few lines before.

What is especially remarkable about Congreve's dramatic prose is the way in which its rhythms, its vocabulary and its idiom always suit the character who is speaking. Many dramatists succeed in distinguishing some of their characters by giving them tricks of speech; but Congreve is unique among dramatists since the Restoration in his ability to distinguish all his characters in his last two plays by their manner of speech. This is a matter which can be checked by listening to a gramophone record or a radio performance; there is never the least doubt as to which character is talking. Congreve had an extraordinary power of mimicry, an extraordinary ability to speak through the mouths of all his characters, old and young, male and female, good and evil, wise and foolish. This is a quality of which too little has been made. Of course, as he tells us, 'the distance of the Stage requires the Figure represented to be something larger than the Life'; and, he might have added, more eloquent than in real life. Even his fools are sometimes witty, as Pope saw; but Congreve defended himself from the charge that they speak out of character by pointing out that,

The saying of Humorous Things, does not distinguish Characters; For every Person in a Comedy may be allow'd to speak them. From a Witty Man they are expected; and even a *Fool* may be permitted to stumble on 'em by chance.

Witwoud, for example, 'a fool with a good memory', is shown striving to be witty by churning out fashionable similitudes, but his memory furnishes him with at least one genuinely witty remark. So, in *Love for Love*, the nautical idiom of Ben—he uses thirty nautical images on his first appearance—the astrological patter of Foresight, the high-pitched fopperies of Tattle, the adolescent gaucherie of Miss Prue, the down-to-earth wit of Jeremy, are all perfectly distinguishable without the need of speech-prefixes. The prose is essentially dramatic: it needs to be spoken, and the actor who keeps Congreve's rhythm automatically registers his points.

Horace Walpole has some remarks which are relevant here.[1] Congreve, he says,

is undoubtedly the most witty author that ever existed. Though sometimes his wit seems the effort of intention, and, though an effort, never failed;

[1] *Works*, II, p. 316.

it was so natural, that, if he split it into ever so many characters, it was a polypus that soon grew perfect in each individual. We may blame the universality of wit in all his personages, but nobody can say which ought to have less. It assimilated with whatever character it was poured into.

Walpole goes on to say that Congreve's

gentlemen, ladies old or young, his footmen, nay his coxcombs (for they are not fools but puppies) have as much wit, and wit as much their own, as his men of most parts and best understandings. No character drops a sentence that would be proper in any other mouth.

After illustrating this, Walpole proceeds to complain of the un-naturalness of the comedies

because four assemblages of different persons could never have so much wit as Congreve has bestowed on them. We want breath or attention to follow their repartees; and are so charmed with what every body says, that we have not leisure to be interested in what any body does.

In the end, therefore, Walpole regards Congreve as an unsatis-factory dramatist. The characters are all so witty that we cannot be emotionally involved in what happens to them.

We even do not believe that a company who seem to meet only to show their wit, can have any other object in view. Their very vices seem affected, only to furnish subject for gaiety . . . For these reasons, though they are something more, I can scarce allow Congreve's to be true comedies. No man would be corrected, if sure that his wit would make his vices or ridicules overlooked.

Walpole's recognition of the way in which Congreve adapts his wit to his different characters is so just, that one is surprised that he should regard the total result of Congreve's art as unnatural, or that he should suppose that we cannot laugh at the witticisms of a Tattle or a Witwoud while we laugh also at the characters who speak the lines.

   In *Love for Love* even the minor characters are alive, whereas in *The Double Dealer* the important character of Lord Touchwood had been somewhat wooden. In another respect *Love for Love* shows an advance on Congreve's previous plays and, indeed, it is this quality which has made some critics place it above *The Way of the World*: it acts even better than it reads. From the theatrical point of view, there is not a weak scene in the play, from the exposition by

Jeremy and Valentine to the marriage of Tattle and Mrs Frail. Such scenes as the exposure of Tattle, the quarrel between Sir Sampson and Foresight, Ben's abortive courtship of Miss Prue, Scandal's pretence that Foresight is ill, and Valentine's pretended madness are inevitably successful on the stage; and the way Mrs Frail turns the tables on her sister is one of the most effective scenes in the whole range of English comedy:

Mrs Foresight . . . You never were at the *World's-End*?
Mrs Frail No.
Mrs Foresight You deny it positively to my Face.
Mrs Frail Your Face, what's Your Face?
Mrs Foresight No matter for that, it's as good a Face as yours.
Mrs Frail Not by a Dozen Years wearing.—But I do deny it positively to Your Face then.
Mrs Foresight I'll allow you now to find fault with my Face; for I'll swear your Impudence has put me out of Countenance:—But look you here now,—where did you lose this Gold Bodkin?—Oh Sister, Sister!
Mrs Frail My Bodkin!
Mrs Foresight Nay, 'tis Yours, look at it.
Mrs Frail Well, if you go to that, where did you find this Bodkin?—Oh Sister, Sister!—Sister every way.

Fanny Burney admitted[1] that the play was 'fraught with wit and entertainment', but she assumed that no lady could approve of it. Its defence was put into the mouth of the robust Captain:

'What, I suppose it is not sentimental enough!' cried the Captain, 'or else it is too good for them; for I'll maintain it's one of the best comedies in our Language, and has more wit in one scene than there is in all the new plays put together.'

Congreve's next play, *The Mourning Bride*, much admired by his contemporaries, and more often acted throughout the eighteenth century than the comedies, strange as it may seem, is outside the scope of this book. Before his next comedy, Collier had fired his broadside and Congreve had replied with a pamphlet which is often spoken of as ineffective, but which appears to be restrained, sensible and witty. *The Way of the World* was written in the autumn of 1699 after Congreve had been a guest in Northamptonshire of the Earl of Montagu, whose conversation, he said, was the cause of the improvement in his dialogue:

[1] *Evelina*, xx.

If it has hapned in any part of this Comedy, that I have gain'd a Turn of Stile, or Expression more Correct, or at least more Corrigible than in those which I have formerly written, I must, with equal Pride and Gratitude, ascribe it to the Honour of your Lordship's admitting me into your Conversation, and that of a Society where everybody else was so well worthy of you, in your Retirement last Summer from the Town.

But, of course, we are not expected to take very seriously the flattery of an epistle dedicatory. The refinement of style observable in *The Way of the World* owed nothing to Lord Montagu or his guests.

The play was not so immediately successful as *Love for Love*, nor has it ever been so popular with audiences. It is not difficult to see why. The first act contains no action, and there is a great deal of discussion of characters we do not meet until later in the play, Millamant not appearing until the middle of Act II and Lady Wishfort, who provides the broadest comedy, not until the third act. Some allusions in the opening scenes are likely to be obscure or even misleading at a first hearing. When Mirabell, for example, hints that Mrs Marwood is Fainall's mistress, an audience would have to be very quick on the uptake to take the hint:

> You pursue the Argument with a distrust that seems to be unaffected, and confesses you are conscious of a Concern for which the Lady is more indebted to you, than your Wife.

It would be impossible for an audience to gather in Act I that Mirabell's uncle was an impostor, and that he was to court Lady Wishfort rather than Millamant. But such difficulties do not arise after a first hearing, and may indeed give ironical undertones to the dialogue.

The plot certainly is a stumbling-block to readers of the play—though not necessarily to audiences—and this has led to an exclusive interest in the scenes in which the plot is of minor importance. Yet, as two recent critics have shown, this is likely to lead to a distorted understanding of the play.[1] They argue that the theme of the play, implicit in the Horatian epigraphs, is 'the danger of losing fame and fortune through the exposure of adultery' and that the plot 'is primarily a legacy conflict centering in Lady Wishfort and the four adulterers'. This, and the contrast between Fainall and Marwood on the one hand, and Mirabell and Mrs Fainall on the other, is as important thematically as the wooing of Millamant.

[1] Paul and Miriam Mueschke, *A New View of Congreve's Way of the World* (1958), pp. 9–10.

The play is fundamentally more serious than *Love for Love* and the dialogue and characterisation are continuously brilliant and more subtle. Congreve avows in his Dedication that he was aiming at greater subtlety:

Those Characters which are meant to be ridicul'd in most of our Comedies, are of Fools so gross, that in my humble Opinion, they should rather disturb than divert the well-natured and reflecting Part of an Audience; they are rather Objects of Charity than Contempt; and instead of moving our Mirth, they ought very often to excite our Compassion. This Reflection moved me to design some Characters, which should appear ridiculous not so much thro' a natural Folly (which is incorrigible, and therefore not proper for the Stage) as thro' an affected Wit; a Wit, which at the same time that it is affected, is also false.

He goes on to complain that some of his audience failed to distinguish between a Witwoud and a Truewit.

This is a curious passage, for the only character to whom these remarks apply is Witwoud himself. Petulant can hardly be described as a wit; Fainall is evil, but not affected; Sir Wilfull is rustic and unaffected; Lady Wishfort is affected in her speech, and eminently ridiculous, but no one would think of her as a wit. Millamant is certainly affected, but no one could pretend that her wit is false. Congreve was attempting to rival Terence of whom he writes in the dedication—alluding no doubt to the defective taste of his own audience: 'The purity of his Stile, the Delicacy of his Turns, and the Justness of his Characters, were all of them Beauties, which the greater Part of his Audience were incapable of tasting'.

The characterisation depends less on exaggeration than it had in Congreve's earlier comedies, though even here, of course, 'the distance of the Stage requires the Figures represented to be something larger than the Life'. Lady Wishfort, indeed, especially in the Sir Rowland scenes, is a figure of farce, though not without pathos; and Sir Wilfull's rusticity arouses sympathetic laughter. The scenes range from these to others which represent the high-water mark of the comedy of manners.

In the opinion of Thomas H. Fujimura, whose book contains one of the best appreciations of Congreve, the comparative unpopularity of *The Way of the World* was due neither to the slowness of the first act, nor to the weakness of the plot which is 'actually superior to that of . . . *The Old Batchelor*', but rather to the sententiousness of Mirabell:[1]

[1] op. cit., pp. 185–7.

he is the Restoration rake in the process of being transformed into a Wit of the age of sense and sensibility. His predominant characteristic as a Truewit is his judgment rather than fancy, and he is more addicted to *sententiae* than to similitudes . . . He is capable of finely balanced phrases, but his remarks are characterised by subtlety of thought and elegance of expression rather than by striking figures of speech . . . [He] is not so attractive a figure as Valentine, for the playful attitude of the Truewit is sobering into a concern with the sound conduct of life. If there is a flaw in Mirabell, it is not his supposed cynicism, but his sobriety.

But, although it is true that Mirabell is a more mature and sober character than previous Restoration heroes, Mr Fujimura seems to have been misled by the thesis of his book to demand that a hero of the Comedy of Wit should be a witty libertine. It is the pretender after wit, Witwoud, who indulges in a frantic search for similitudes: the Truewit in this play is witty at times, but it is no longer his *raison d'être* to be so, and he has few similitudes. He can still be devastatingly witty:

Mirabell A Fool, and your Brother, *Witwoud*!
Witwoud Ay, ay, my half Brother. My half Brother he is, no nearer, upon Honour.
Mirabell Then 'tis possible he may be but half a Fool.

But his more characteristic mode of expression is to be found in his meditation on Beauty as the Lover's gift or in his account of how he tried to cure himself of his love for Millamant:

Fainall For a passionate Lover, methinks you are a Man somewhat too discerning in the Failings of your Mistress.
Mirabell And for a discerning Man, somewhat too passionate a Lover; for I like her with all her Faults; nay, like her for her Faults. Her Follies are so natural, or so artful, that they become her; and those Affectations which in another Woman wou'd be odious, serve but to make her more agreeable. I'll tell thee, *Fainall*, she once us'd me with that Insolence, that in Revenge I took her to pieces; sifted her and separated her Failings; I study'd 'em, and got 'em by rote. The Catalogue was so large, that I was not without hopes, one Day or other to hate her heartily: To which end I so us'd my self to think of 'em, that at length, contrary to my Design and Expectation, they gave me every Hour less and less disturbance; 'till in a few Days it become habitual to me, to remember 'em without being displeas'd. They are now grown as familiar to me as my own Frailties; and in all probability in a little time longer I shall like 'em as well.

Audiences, like Mirabell, love Millamant with all her faults, and even for her faults. In this they are wiser than some of the critics. Professor L. C. Knights, in his famous attack on Restoration comedy, spoke of Millamant in a way which seems to exhibit a misunderstanding of what Congreve was doing, as well as an imperfect understanding of the character. He complains that she 'expects to draw vitality from the excitement of incessant solicitation'; that she shares with unattractive characters 'a disproportionate belief in the pleasure of a chase', and that her way of life 'is never for a moment enlivened by the play of genuine intelligence'.

As we have seen, Mirabell—and Congreve too—is aware of Millamant's faults. But, oddly enough, none of the faults listed by Knights can reasonably be ascribed to her. It is necessary, for example, to realise why she wishes not to be 'freed from the agreeable Fatigues of Sollicitation'. She lives in a society in which constancy is regarded as a bore, and in which marriage ends in disillusionment. She wishes to avoid what Swift's Stella was to describe as the common lot of women:

> Before the thirti'th year of life,
> A maid forlorn, or hated wife.

Hazlitt thought Millamant was 'nothing but a fine lady', and Meredith said she was 'a type of the superior ladies who do not think'. Both critics are surely mistaken. Millamant's wit, like that of Rosalind and Beatrice, is a sign of intelligence; and although affectation and coquetry usually indicate a frigid temperament, Millamant's affectation is the cloak of affection, and her coquetry conceals a nature capable of a whole-hearted love. She can act the fine lady to perfection, she can pose as a woman who makes wit the be-all and end-all of her life, but fundamentally she is a sensitive girl in an insensitive society.

As Fujimura says[1]

> her whimsical wit is a shield she holds up against the world . . . In addition to her judgment and sense, Mrs Millamant has a real capacity for deep feeling, and her love for Mirabell is all the more impressive because she has such a mastery over it.

That Millamant is genuinely in love, and not a coquette, is made perfectly clear when, just after the bargaining scene, she confesses to

---

[1] op. cit., pp. 189–91. The same point was made in my article in the *Leeds University Review* (1949).

her friend: 'Well, if *Mirabell* shou'd not make a good Husband, I am a lost thing—for I find I love him violently'.

Angelica, the most philosophical of Congreve's heroines, and without any of the affectations of Belinda or Millamant, refers obliquely to her fear of disillusionment, when she tells Valentine, who has been feigning madness:

> Wou'd any thing, but a Madman, complain of Uncertainty? Uncertainty and Expectation are the Joys of Life. Security is an insipid thing, and the overtaking and possessing of a Wish, discovers the Folly of the Chase. Never let us know one another better; for the Pleasure of a Masquerade is done, when we come to show our Faces.

It is in *The Way of the World* that the fear of disillusionment in marriage is treated most fully. Such fears had been expressed by some of Shakespeare's heroines—by Rosalind, for example, when in the guise of Ganymede she tells Orlando: 'Men are April when they woo, December when they wed'. But what in Rosalind is just a joke, in Millamant becomes almost her dominant mood. The manners of society determine the nature of the comedy: and in the play in which Millamant appears the example of Mrs Fainall or Mrs Marwood is not encouraging to anyone who would embark on the dangerous seas of matrimony, even though Millamant confesses, though not to Mirabell, that she loves him violently. Because of her fears, Millamant makes Mirabell agree not to use endearments and to behave in public as if they were not married at all.

But the most subtle way by which Millamant conveys her anxiety 'on the very Verge of Matrimony' is by her quotations from Waller and Suckling. Congreve was not entirely original in his method. Belinda's quotation is a means of characterising her—'Oh Gad! I have a great Passion for Cowley . . . Ah so fine! So extreamly fine! So every thing in the World that I like'—and Etherege made his Dorimant copy Rochester's trick of quoting Waller. But, as Bonamy Dobrée pointed out, though he suggested that Congreve was expecting too much from his audience, all Millamant's quotations are concerned with the disadvantages of fruition. Almost all the cavalier poets wrote poems in praise of platonic love and against fruition. Lord Herbert wrote that strong passion in youth 'is not yet affection, but disease' and in another poem he refrains from pressing his suit lest his mistress should afterwards regret her compliance. Suckling protests that

> Women enjoyed (whate'er before they've been)
> Are like romances read, or sights once seen;
> Fruition's dull, and spoils the play much more
> Than if one read or knew the plot before;
> 'Tis expectation makes a blessing dear,
> Heaven were not heaven, if we knew what it were.

In another poem Suckling goes further: indeed, he goes so far that we must assume he was being ironical:

> Oh, what a stroke 'twould be, sure I should die,
> Should I but hear my mistress once say Ay.

Henry King declares that we may as well

> Enjoy our Love and yet preserve Desire,
> As warm our hands by putting out the fire.

And Cowley tells his mistress:

> No; thou'rt a fool, I'll swear, if e'er thou grant
> Much of my *Veneration* thou must want,
> When once thy *Kindness* puts my *Ignorance* out;
> For a *learn'd Age* is always less devout.

Millamant's first quotation—

> There never yet was woman made
> Nor shall, but to be curs'd—

are lines taken from one of Suckling's poems, which purports to discuss the promiscuity of women, but which goes on to imply the inconstancy of men. She then quotes the first stanza of another of Suckling's poems:

> I prithee spare me, gentle Boy,
> Press me no more for that slight Toy,
> That foolish Trifle of a Heart;
> I swear it will not do its part,
> Tho' thou dost thine, employ'st thy Power and Art.

Some members of Congreve's original audience would know how the poem continues. Suckling confesses that his gallantries are loveless and heartless. He will not even bother to court the women who attract him. He will 'rudely call for the last course before the rest' and after he has been successful, he will lose interest in the woman:

> Men rise away, and scarce say grace,
> Or civilly once thank the face
> That did invite, but seek another place.

Millamant's other quotations are from Waller's 'Story of Phoebus and Daphne, Applied'. She quotes the first line while Mrs Fainall is on the stage, and the third line on the exit of Sir Wilful Witwoud a few minutes later. She is, of course, quoting from memory, not reading from a book as I have seen one actress doing:

> Like *Phoebus* sung the no less am'rous Boy

Mirabell, entering at this moment, completes the couplet:

> Like *Daphne* she, as lovely and as coy!

Mirabell thus demonstrates that he understands the allusion and, perhaps, that theirs is a marriage of true minds. Waller's poem, like Marvell's which imitated it, is on the subject of sublimation.

> Apollo hunted Daphne so
> Only that she might laurel grow,

said Marvell; and Waller's poet, Thyrsis,

> Like *Phoebus* thus, acquiring unsought praise,
> He catch'd at Love, and fill'd his arms with bays.

The implication in both cases is that it is better for poets, if not for all men, not to consummate their love.

All the poems are written from the masculine point of view, and it is a curious result of libertinism that they should all be opposed to fruition. The reason, as we have seen, is that the poets believe that desire dies with its satisfaction; and this accounts for the ambivalent feelings about marriage the heroes of many Restoration comedies have and also the reluctance of the more sensitive heroines to risk disillusionment. Millamant, moreover, knows that her cousin is Mirabell's cast-off mistress,[1] and that she is treated badly by her husband. In the society of her time, and according to the way of the world, she has reason to fear. It may be added, in view of Knights' statement, that the aptness of Millamant's quotations is enough to prove that she had 'genuine intelligence', and that she was a match for Mirabell, the character in all Congreve's plays which comes closest to being a self-portrait.

The actual bargain scene, where both Mirabell and Millamant pretend they are not desperately in love, is in a sense traditional. Beatrice and Benedick have something of the same attitude at the end of *Much Ado about Nothing*. The conditions themselves, as Kathleen Lynch has shown,[2] can be paralleled in D'Urfé's *Astrée* and in the scene between Florimel and Celadon in Dryden's *Secret Love* discussed in Chapter 3. In spite of obvious resemblances, the enormous superiority of Congreve's scene is apparent. Dryden's lines are generalised, and they could have been spoken by almost any lovers on the verge of matrimony between 1660 and 1710; Congreve's are all perfectly in character, rich in detail, and continuously witty; and the scene gains from the juxtaposition of Sir Wilfull's abortive proposal. The absurdity of supposing that Millamant and he could ever make a match of it throws into relief the more civilised qualities of Mirabell.

No dramatist has equalled Congreve in the creation of character by diction and rhythm:

Millamant My dear Liberty, shall I leave thee? My faithful Solitude, my darling Contemplation, must I bid you then Adieu? Ay-h adieu— My morning thoughts, agreeable wakings, indolent slumbers, all ye *douceurs*, ye *Someils du Matin*, adieu—I can't do't, 'tis more than Impossible—positively *Mirabell*, I'll lie a Bed in a morning as long as I please.

Mirabell Then I'll get up in a morning as early as I please.

Millamant Ah! Idle Creature, get up when you will—And d'ye hear, I won't be call'd names after I'm Married; positively I won't be called Names.

Mirabell Names!

Millamant Ay, as Wife, Spouse, my Dear, Joy, Jewel, Love, Sweet-heart, and the rest of that Nauseous Cant, in which Men and their Wives are so fulsomly familiar—I shall never bear that—Good *Mirabell* don't let us be familiar or fond, nor kiss before folks, like my Lady

---

[1] Mirabell tells Mrs Fainall: 'You shou'd have just so much disgust for your Husband, as may be sufficient to make you relish your Lover'. But the impression we get is that their affair is a thing of the past.

[2] See p. 44 above.

> *Fadler* and Sir *Francis* . . . Let us never Visit together, nor go to a
> Play together, but let us be very strange and well bred: let us be as
> strange as if we had been married a great while; and as well bred as
> if we were not married at all.

This is one example of the way Congreve, writing within well-
worn conventions, was able to transmute the commonplace into
great dramatic dialogue. One other example may be given, where
Congreve was certainly playing variations on a theme of Etherege.
In *The Man of Mode*, as we have seen, Dorimant upbraids Mrs
Loveit for encouraging fools. So Mirabell complains that Millamant
had denied him a private audience on the previous evening:

> Unkind. You had the leisure to entertain a Herd of Fools; Things
> who visit you from their excessive Idleness; bestowing on your
> easiness that time which is the incumbrance of their Lives. How can
> you find delight in such Society? It is impossible they should admire
> you, they are not capable; Or if they were, it shou'd be to you as a
> Mortification; for sure to please a Fool is some degree of Folly.
> *Millamant* I please my self—Besides, sometimes to converse with Fools
> is for my Health.
> *Mirabell* Your Health! Is there a worse Disease than the Conversation of
> Fools?
> *Millamant* Yes, the Vapours; Fools are Physick for it, next to *Assa-
> foetida*.

The style of the play is beautifully varied and the voices are all
perfectly distinct. The idea that all Congreve's characters talk in
the same style is one which is difficult to understand, much less
accept. It was not Congreve's fault that some of his audience mistook
his Witwoud for a Truewit, for nothing could be more different
than the gushing, effeminate manner of Witwoud, with his frantic
pursuit of similitudes, and the grave, poetical meditations of Mirabell;
and both characters are equally distinguished by the prose they speak
from the surly Petulant, and the rustic Sir Wilfull. The female
voices are varied also. There is what Meredith called the 'boudoir
Billingsgate' of Lady Wishfort as she sacks Foible and her pretentious
diction in her scene with Sir Rowland—so much more subtle than
Mrs Malaprop:

> You must not attribute my yielding to any sinister appetite, or
> Indigestion of Widdow-hood; Nor Impute my Complacency, to any
> Lethargy of Continence—I hope you do not think me prone to any
> iteration of Nuptials.

As a contrast, there are the elaborate pretences of Marwood and
Mrs Fainall, as they seek to read each other's hearts at the beginning
of Act II, the corrosive bitterness of Marwood when alone, or the
malicious exchanges between Marwood and Millamant:

> The Town has found it . . . What has it found? That *Mirabell* loves
> me is no more a Secret, than it is a Secret that you discover'd it to
> my Aunt, or than the Reason why you discover'd it is a Secret.

Mrs Marwood You are nettl'd.
Millamant You're mistaken. Ridiculous!
Mrs Marwood Indeed my Dear, you'll tear another Fan, if you don't
mitigate those violent Airs.
Millamant O silly! Ha, ha, ha. I cou'd laugh immoderately. Poor *Mirabell*!
His Constancy to me has quite destroy'd his Complaisance for all
the World beside. I swear, I never enjoin'd it him, to be so coy—If
I had the Vanity to think he wou'd obey me; I wou'd command him
to shew more Gallantry—'Tis hardly well bred to be so particular on
one Hand, and so insensible on the other. But I despair to prevail,
and so let him follow his own way. Ha, ha, ha. Pardon me, dear
Creature, I must laugh, Ha, ha, ha; tho' I grant you 'tis a little
barbarous, Ha, ha, ha.
Mrs Marwood What pity 'tis, so much fine Raillery, and deliver'd with
so significant Gesture, shou'd be so unhappily directed to miscarry.
Millamant Hæ? Dear Creature I ask your Pardon—I swear I did not
mind you.
Mrs Marwood Mr *Mirabell* and you both, may think it a Thing impos-
sible, when I shall tell him, by telling you—
Millamant O Dear, what? for it is the same thing if I hear it—Ha, ha, ha.
Mrs Marwood That I detest him, hate him, Madam.
Millamant O Madam, why so do I—And yet the Creature loves me, Ha,
ha, ha. How can one forbear laughing to think of it—I am a Sybil if
I am not amaz'd to think what he can see in me. I'll take my Death,
I think you are the handsomer—And within a Year or two as young.
If you cou'd but stay for me, I shou'd overtake you—But that cannot
be—Well, that Thought makes me Melancholly—Now I'll be sad.

The song chosen by Millamant to entertain Marwood with is the
last twist of the knife. The joy of love consists in triumph over a
rival:

> But 'tis the Glory to have pierc'd a Swain,
> For whom inferior Beauties sigh'd in vain.
>   Then I alone the Conquest prize
>   When I insult a Rival's Eyes:

> If there's Delight in Love, 'tis when I see
> That Heart which others bleed for, bleed for me.

No one could have any difficulty in distinguishing between the tones of the six women of the play. Indeed, in the great scene in Act II where Millamant arrives, decked out like Dalila in *Samson Agonistes*—'full sail, with fan spread and streamers out'—there are five characters, each with a distinctive mode of speech.

Mrs Fainall asks why Millamant was so long:

Mrs Fainall You were dress'd before I came abroad.
Millamant Ay, that's true—O but then I had—*Mincing*, what had I? Why was I so long.
Mincing O Mem, your Laship staid to peruse a Pecquet of Letters.
Millamant O ay, Letters—I had Letters—I am persecuted with Letters— I hate Letters—No Body knows how to write Letters: and yet one has 'em, one does not know why—They serve one to pin up one's Hair.
Witwoud Is that the way? Pray, Madam, do you pin up your Hair with all your Letters? I find I must keep Copies.
Millamant Only with those in Verse, Mr *Witwoud*. I never pin up my Hair with Prose. I fancy ones Hair wou'd not curl if it were pinn'd up with Prose.

The distinctive voice of Mirabell is heard a few lines later:

> Ay, ay, suffer your Cruelty to ruin the Object of your Power, to destroy your Lover—And then how lost a Thing you'll be! Nay, 'tis true: You are no longer handsome when you've lost your Lover; your Beauty dies upon the Instant: for Beauty is the Lover's Gift; 'tis he bestows your Charms—Your Glass is all a Cheat. The Ugly and the Old, whom the Looking-Glass mortifies, yet after Commendation can be flatter'd by it, and discover Beauties in it: For that reflects our Praises, rather than your Face.

We can admire the vowel-music of this passage, if we wish; but the real point about it is that it is a perfect revelation of character.

Some dramatic critics, shutting their eyes to Congreve's success in the theatre in our own time, persist in the belief that the academic critic is apt to be seduced by the 'beauty' of Congreve's prose into believing he was a good dramatist. But this misses the point. Congreve's plays are meant to be enjoyed in the theatre, rather than to be savoured in the study, as Virginia Woolf's praise indicates.[1]

[1] *The Moment* (1947), p. 32.

Never was any prose so quick. Miraculously pat, on the spot, each speaker
caps the last, without fumbling or hesitation; their minds are full charged;
it seems as if they had to rein themselves in, bursting with energy as they
are, alive and alert to their finger tips. It is we who fumble, make irrelevant
observations, until the illusion takes hold of us, and what with the
rhythm of the speech and the indescribable air of tension, of high breeding
that pervades it, the world of the stage becomes the real world and the
other, outside the play, but the husk and cast-off clothing. The impression
is conveyed by the curl of a phrase on the ear; by speed; by stillness. It is
as impossible to analyse Congreve's prose as to distinguish the elements
which make the summer air. But then, since words have meaning, we
notice here a sudden depth beneath the surface, a meaning not grasped
but felt, and then come to realise something not merely dazzling in this
world, but natural, for all its wit; even familiar, and traditional. It has a
coarseness, a humour, something like Shakespeare's; a toppling imagination that heaps image upon image; a lightning swiftness of apprehension
that snatches a dozen meanings and compacts them into one.

It is the wonderful speakability of Congreve's prose, which is his
greatest triumph. If the actor keeps the rhythms, and stresses the
right words, the meaning is easy to follow. This is one reason why
actors who have appeared in a Congreve comedy find it difficult
and disappointing to appear afterwards in a prose comedy by any
other dramatist.

Even those critics who admit that Congreve's plays—and especially
The Way of the World—are incomparably the finest examples of
the comedy of manners, and certainly superior in most ways to *The
School for Scandal* or *She Stoops to Conquer*, are apt to complain of
the artificiality of the *genre*. It is no longer possible to accept Lamb's
ingenious argument, which he never intended to be taken seriously,
that the plays are fantasies about an imaginary world; they reflect
in a highly polished mirror the society of Congreve's day. The truly
artificial comedies (as Dobrée has remarked) are the sentimental
plays of Congreve's successors. But, it is argued, the world with
which they deal is a narrow one, the characters are 'heartless', and
we do not much care what happens to them. Schelling spoke of
Congreve's 'brilliant, soulless dramatic art'[1] and Henry Ten Eyck
Perry, while admitting that the surface of his plays is dazzling,
complained of the lack beneath:[2]

it is only too evident that Congreve never really understood the funda-

[1] *English Drama*, p. 307.
[2] *The Comic Spirit in Restoration Drama* (Ed. 1962), p. 80.

mental principles of human behaviour . . . He is, after all, only a professional funny man.

It is difficult to answer such strange misunderstandings both of the nature of comedy and of Congreve's art. But it may at least be said that the world of his plays is not so narrow as it is sometimes painted, and that we are not bounded by the walls of a fashionable drawing-room, as we are, for example, in *Le Misanthrope*. The outside world—in the shape of Ben, Sir Wilfull, 'bouncing Margery', Trapland's widow, Pumple-Nose the Attorney—is continually breaking in; and there is a great social gulf between Lord Touchwood and Fondlewife, for example, or between Miss Prue and Millamant.

It is equally important to emphasise that the central characters are not heartless, although—as we have seen with regard to Mirabell and Millamant—they pretend to be less in love than they are. That ladies and gentlemen are also men and women is the chief point of the play. The characters for whom our sympathies are engaged are the most sympathetic ones in the plays; and if we read them in chronological order, we notice a gradual change of attitude on the part of the dramatist. We are not asked to condemn Bellmour's promiscuity very seriously; but Congreve was criticised for his satire of female frailty in *The Double Dealer*, and Valentine's prodigal past is one reason why Angelica hesitates to marry him. All Congreve's heroines are chaste. The adultery of Fainall with Mrs Marwood is condemned; and if the relationship of Mirabell and Mrs Fainall is condoned, one has only to compare it with Dorimant's treatment of his former mistresses to see how much more civilised Congreve is than Etherege.

The accusation that Congreve's heroes are heartless and cynical has rubbed off on the dramatist himself. It is ironical that a man who was the embodiment of sensibility, a man whose contemporaries were unanimous in praising for the sweetness of his manners and the kindness of his heart, should be regarded as a monster of cold cynicism. Congreve, we are told, did not believe in faith or honour. He 'watches the corruption of society with an amused detachment, and is resolved to be content if it is only graceful'.[1]

It should be remembered that Congreve was still a young man when *The Way of the World* was performed—just over thirty—and that during the remaining thirty years of his life he wrote nothing

[1] J. W. Krutch, *Comedy and Conscience after the Restoration* (1924), pp. 46–7 (but as the words were written in 1920, the author may have altered his views afterwards).

of importance: part of a translation of a Molière farce, a couple of odes, a couple of libretti. Why he gave up writing comedies is still a matter for debate. He suffered a good deal in later years from indifferent health; he may have been disappointed by the cool reception of *The Way of the World*: this is the implication of these remarks by Dennis:[1]

There is a Gentleman, the living Ornament of the Comick Scene, who after he had for several Years entertain'd the Town, with that Wit and Humour, and Art and Vivacity, which are so becoming of the Comick Stage, produc'd at last a Play, which besides that it was equal to most of the former in those pleasant Humours which the Laughers so much require, had some certain Scenes in it, which were writ with so much Grace and Delicacy, that they alone were worth an entire Comedy. What was the Event? The Play was hiss'd by Barbarous Fools in the Acting; and an impertinent Trifle was brought on after it, which was acted with vast Applause. Which rais'd so much Indignation in the foresaid Writer, that he quitted the Stage in Disdain, and Comedy left it with him.

It has also been suggested that there may have been some kind of break with Anne Bracegirdle, the actress for whom Congreve had written the parts of Cynthia, Angelica, Almeria (in *The Mourning Bride*) and Millamant; and he may have felt that he had said all he wanted to say in a way that could hardly be bettered. But it is fairly safe to assume that he felt out of sympathy with the temper of the new century. As Pope said, Congreve was 'Ultimus Romanorum'. The success of Collier's diatribe was bad enough; the applause which greeted *Love's Last Shift* was worse, and it adumbrated the triumph of sentimental comedy. Congreve cannot have been very surprised that audiences found *The Way of the World* too astringent; and when Cibber produced *The Careless Husband*, Congreve told Kealley that 'the ridiculous town for the most part' liked it. 'But', he added, 'there are some that know better'. It is lamentable to think that those who know better have seldom been in a majority since the end of the seventeenth century; and that more than one modern critic has declared that 'Congreve is essentially an author who does not know how to write for the stage.'

[1] J. Dennis, *Critical Works*, Vol. 2, Ed. E. N. Hooker (1943), p. 121.

8

SIR JOHN VANBRUGH

Vanbrugh, more famous as the architect of Blenheim Palace and Castle Howard than as a dramatist, was born in 1664, served in the army as a young man and spent some time as a prisoner in the Bastille, where he is said to have sketched some scenes which developed later into *The Provok'd Wife*. All his plays were written between 1695 and 1705. They included adaptations from Molière and other French dramatists, and one of Fletcher's *The Pilgrim*. The only one of these of any importance is the brilliant anglicisation of Dancourt's *Les Bourgeoises à la Mode*, entitled *The Confederacy*. Vanbrugh's original plays are few in number. Besides *The Provok'd Wife*, there is only *The Relapse*, a sequel to Colley Cibber's *Love's Last Shift*, and four acts of *A Journey to London* which Cibber completed as *The Provoked Husband*.

The success of *Love's Last Shift* had social, rather than literary, causes. Audiences felt vaguely that the comedy of manners which they had enjoyed for a generation deserved some at least of Collier's strictures—it was too bawdy and its immoral hero was rewarded in the last act with the hand of the heroine. Colley Cibber hit on the expedient of making the rake repent in Act V. The moralists, the rakes, and the sentimentalists in the audience were pleased; but the means by which Loveless is brought to repentance are somewhat absurd from the realistic point of view. He has deserted his wife, not because he loved another but because of the fashionable view that no gentleman can continue to love his wife—the subtitle of the play is 'The Fool in Fashion'—and after some years abroad is told that she has died, as Bertram is told of Helena's death in *All's Well that Ends Well.* Amanda, like Helena, contrives to sleep with her husband without his knowing it. On the following morning, he sees Amanda's face, but still does not recognise her. When she reveals her identity, Loveless is shamed into repentance, the more easily as he has been forced to admit that a wife can give as much pleasure as a mistress. We are told that the original audience wept copiously at the reform of Loveless and his reconciliation with his wife. The sentiments are admirable, but the expression of them is embarrassingly sentimental:

> Since then you have allow'd a Woman may be virtuous,—How will you excuse the Man who leaves the Bosom of a Wife so qualify'd, for the abandon'd Pleasures of deceitful Prostitutes? ruins her Fortune! contemns her Counsel! loaths her Bed, and leaves her to the lingring Miseries of Despair and Love: While, in return of all these Wrongs, she, his poor forsaken Wife meditates no Revenge but what her piercing Tears, and secret Vows to Heav'n for his Conversion, yield her: Yet still loves on, is constant and unshaken to the last! Can you believe that such a Man can live without the Stings of Conscience, and yet be Master of his Senses! Conscience! did you ne'er feel the Checks of it? Did it never, never tell you of your broken Vows?
>
> *Lov.* That you shou'd ask me this, confounds my Reason:—And yet your Words are utter'd with such a powerful Accent, they have awaken'd my Soul, and strike my thoughts with Horror and Remorse.—
>
> *[Stands in a fix'd Posture.]*
>
> *Am.* Then let me strike you nearer, deeper yet:—But arm your mind with gentle Pity first, or I am lost for ever.

It will be observed that Cibber, whether accidentally or by design, drops into blank verse in emotional passages; and the same thing, as we shall see, is apt to happen with Vanbrugh and Farquhar. None of the three dramatists is a tolerable versifier and the results are always unfortunate.

At the end of the play there is a musical interlude in which the praises of married love are sung, and Loveless accepts the moral:

> Oh, *Amanda!* once more receive me to thy Arms; and while I am there, let all the World confess my Happiness. By my Example taught, let every Man, whose Fate has bound him to a marry'd Life, beware of letting loose his wild Desires; For if Experience may be allow'd to judge, I must proclaim the Folly of a wandring Passion. The greatest Happiness we can hope on Earth,

> *And sure the nearest to the Joys above,*
> *Is the chaste Rapture of a virtuous Love.*

Vanbrugh was right to see that there was an element of insincerity
in Cibber's play, and to show in *The Relapse* that rakes who repent
in Act V may find it difficult to keep their good resolutions. There
was, however, one character in *Love's Last Shift* uncontaminated by
the prevailing sentimentality, namely Sir Novelty Fashion, the part
played by Cibber himself. The character was in a direct line of
descent from Sir Fopling Flutter, but sufficiently individualised to
make it an excellent acting part.

Narcissa . . . But you, Sir *Novelty*, are a true Original, the very Pink of
Fashion; I'll warrant you there's not a Milliner in Town but has got
an Estate by you.

Sir Nov. I must confess, Madam, I am for doing good to my Country:
For you see this Suit, Madam—I suppose you are not ignorant what
a hard time the Ribbon-Weavers have had since the late Mourning:
Now my design is to set the poor Rogues up again, by recommending
this sort of Trimming: The Fancy is pretty well for second Mourning
—By the way, Madam, I had fifteen hundred Guineas laid in my Hand,
as a Gratuity, to encourage it: But, i'gad, I refus'd 'em, being too well
acquainted with the Consequence of taking a Bribe in a national
Concern!

Later on, he exclaims:

O Ged, I wou'd not be the ruin of any Lady's Reputation, for the
World. Stop my Vitals! I'm very sorry for 't.

Vanbrugh, when he ennobled Sir Novelty as Lord Foppington, took
over all the characteristics given him by Cibber, including his
pronunciations and his taste for curious oaths, and made him even
funnier by his greater powers of comic invention and by his superior
stylishness. For, as Congreve said—Cibber acknowledged the justice
of the remark—*Love's Last Shift* had a great many things which
were like wit, that in reality were not wit.

Cibber introduced Foppington again into *The Careless Husband*
but in this play the character is less amusing. The play repeats the
situation of *Love's Last Shift*, with a forgiving wife reforming an
erring husband, but in the best scenes Cibber retains much of the
spirit, if not the style, of the writers of the comedy of manners. Lady
Betty, in talking with Lady Easy, is reminiscent of more famous
heroines:

L. Bet. .... I always take Admiration for the best Proof of Beauty, and Beauty certainly is the source of Power, as Power in all creatures is the heighth of Happiness.
L. Ea. At this rate you had rather be thought Beautiful than Good.
L. Bet. As I had rather Command than Obey; The wisest homely Woman can't make a Man of Sense of a Fool, but the veriest Fool of a Beauty, shall make an Ass of a Statesman; so that in short, I can't see a Woman of Spirit has any Business in this World but to dress—and make the Men like her . . . The Men of Sense, my Dear, make the best Fools in the World; their Sincerity and good Breeding throws 'em so entirely into one's Power, and gives one such an agreeable Thirst of using 'em ill, to shew that Power—'tis impossible not to quench it.

Lady Easy warns her about jeopardising her reputation:

L. Ea. At this rate, I don't see you allow Reputation to be at all Essential to a Fine Woman.
L. Bet. Just as much as Honour to a great Man: Power always is above Scandal . . . Indeed, my Dear, that Jewel Reputation is a very fancifull Business; one shall not see one homely creature in Town, but wears it in her Mouth as monstrously as the *Indians* do Bobs at their Lips, and it really becomes 'em just alike.

There are two plots in *The Relapse*, only tenuously related. One concerns Tom Fashion's outwitting of his elder brother, Lord Foppington, by marrying his intended bride Hoyden Clumsey. This particularly shocked Collier. The other concerns Loveless's relapse and his seduction of his wife's friend, Berinthia, while Amanda repulses the advances of Worthy. The characters of this plot are present when Foppington is robbed of his bride and Foppington had tried earlier to make love to Amanda, only to receive a slap in the face; but the two plots are not otherwise linked. In fact the Loveless plot is left in the air. After Loveless has been unfaithful and his wife (despite her knowledge of this) refuses to capitulate to Worthy, we are not given the scene between husband and wife we have a right to expect.

Vanbrugh owes more to Cibber than is generally allowed in his portrait of Lord Foppington, since, as we have seen, the main outlines of the character were sketched in *Love's Last Shift* and since he relied on Cibber's continuing to act the part. His more distant ancestors include Sir Fopling Flutter; but Foppington's vanity and foppishness are united with selfishness and shrewdness.

E

Vanbrugh displays a brilliance and style he never afterwards equalled:

Lord Fop. Far Gad's sake, Madam, haw has your Ladyship been able to subsist thus long, under the Fatigue of a Country Life?

Aman. My Life has been very far from that, my Lord; it has been a very quiet one.

Lord Fop. Why, that the Fatigue I speak of, Madam. For 'tis impossible to be quiet, without thinking: Now thinking is to me the greatest Fatigue in the World.

Aman. Does not your Lordship love reading then?

Lord Fop. Oh, passionately, Madam—But I never think of what I read.

Ber. Why, can your Lordship read without thinking?

Lord Fop. O Lard!—Can your Ladyship pray without Devotion—Madam?

Aman. Well, I must own I think Books the best Entertainment in the World.

Lord Fop. I am so much of your Ladyship's mind, Madam, that I have a private Gallery (where I walk sometimes) is furnished with nothing but Books and Looking-glasses. Madam, I have gilded 'em, and rang'd 'em so prettily, before Gad, it is the most entertaining thing in the World to walk and look upon 'em.

Aman. Nay, I love a neat Library, too; but 'tis, I think, the inside of a Book shou'd recommend it most to us.

Lord Fop. That, I must confess, I am nat altogether so fand of. Far to mind the inside of a Book, is to entertain one's self with the forc'd Product of another Man's Brain. Naw I think a Man of Quality and Breeding may be much better diverted with the Natural Sprauts of his own. But to say the truth, Madam, let a man love reading never so well, when once he comes to know this Tawn, he finds so many better ways of passing the Four and Twenty Hours, that 'twere Ten Thousand pities he shou'd consume his time in that. Far example, Madam, my Life; my Life, Madam, is a perpetual Stream of Pleasure, that glides thro' such a Variety of Entertainments, I believe the wisest of our Ancestors never had the least Conception of any of 'em. I rise, Madam, about Ten a-Clack. I don't rise sooner, because 'tis the worst thing in the World for the Complexion; nat that I pretend to be a Beau; but a Man must endeavour to look wholesome, lest he make so nauseous a Figure in the Side-bax, the Ladies should be compell'd to turn their Eyes upon the Play. So at Ten a-clack, I say, I rise. Naw if I find 'tis a good Day, I resalve to take a turn in the Park, and see the fine Women; so huddle on my Cloaths, and get dressed by One. If it be nasty Weather, I take a turn in the Chocolate-hause: where, as you walk, Madam, you have the prettiest Prospect in the World; you have Looking-glasses all raund you—But I'm afraid I tire the Company.

Ber. Not at all. Pray go on.

Lord Fop. Why then, Ladies, from thence I go to dinner at *Lacket's*, where you are so nicely and delicately serv'd, that, stap me vitals! they shall compose you a Dish, no bigger than a Saucer, shall come to fifty Shillings. Between eating my Dinner (and washing my Mauth, Ladies) I spend my time, till I go to the Play; where, till Nine a-Clack, I entertain myself with looking upon the Company; and usually dispose of one Hour more in leading 'em aut. So there's Twelve of the Four and Twenty pretty well over. The other Twelve, Madam, are disposed of in Two Articles: in the first Four I toast myself drunk, and in t'other Eight I sleep myself sober again. Thus, Ladies, you see my Life is an eternal raund O of Delights.

He is proud to be a fop—'proud to be head of so prevailing a party'; and his final acceptance of defeat is magnificent:

Lord Fop. [*Aside*] Now, for my part, I think the wisest thing a Man can do with an Aking Heart is to put on a serene Countenance; for a Philosophical Air is the most becoming thing in the World to the face of a Person of Quality. I will therefore bear my Disgrace like a Great Man, and let the People see I am above an affront.— [*Aloud*] Dear Tam, since Things are thus fallen aut, prithee give me leave to wish thee Jay; I do it *de bon Coeur*, strike me dumb! You have Marry'd a Woman Beautiful in her Person, Charming in her Ayrs, Prudent in her Canduct, Canstant in her Inclinations, and of a nice Marality, split my Windpipe!

Hazlitt described[1] Foppington as

a most splendid caricature; he is a personification of the foppery and folly of dress and external appearance in full feather. He blazes out and dazzles sober reason with ridiculous ostentation.

Sheridan did not improve on the portrait in *A Trip to Scarborough.*[2]

The Foppington scenes, though the most brilliant, do not constitute the main action of the play. This, as the title signifies, is provided by Loveless's relapse and Amanda's refusal to avenge herself by taking a lover, despite the attraction she feels for Worthy. His proposal to his former mistress that she should act as his bawd, so that her affair with Loveless will not be noticed by Amanda, is set out with considerable verve. Worthy promises to return to Berinthia

[1] *Lectures on the English Comic Writers* (ed. 1910), p. 82.
[2] An adaptation of *The Relapse.*

if she will help him to have 'one short campaign with Amanda':

Ber. Do you then think, Sir, I am old enough to be a Bawd?
Wor. No, but I think you are wise enough to—
Ber. To do what?
Wor. To hoodwink *Amanda* with a Gallant, that she mayn't see who is
    her Husband's Mistress.
Ber. [*Aside*] He has reason: the Hint's a good one.
Wor. Well, Madam, what think you on't?
Ber. I think you are so much a deeper Politician in these Affairs than I
    am, that I ought to have a very great regard to your Advice.
Wor. Then give me leave to put you in mind, that the most easie, safe,
    and pleasant Situation for your own Amour, is the House in which
    you now are; provided you keep *Amanda* from any sort of Suspicion.
    That the way to do that, is to engage her in an Intrigue of her own,
    making yourself her Confidante . . . This is my Scheme, in short;
    which if you follow as you shou'd do (my dear *Berinthia*) we may all
    four pass the Winter very pleasantly.
Ber. Well, I could be glad to have nobody's Sins to answer for but my
    own. But where there is a necessity—
Wor. Right! as you say, where there is a necessity, a Christian is bound
    to help his Neighbour.

This passage, witty as it is, is one of the few of which Jeremy Collier
might justly complain: for Vanbrugh deliberately—if ironically—
called his rake Worthy.

Equally effective is Berinthia's hypocritical pretence that, when
her affair with Loveless is about to be consummated, she is being
raped:

Lov. . . . Therefore, my dear charming Angel, let us make good use of
    our time.
Ber. Heavens! What do you mean?
Lov. Pray what do you think I mean?
Ber. I don't know.
Lov. I'll shew you . . . Come into the Closet, Madam, there's Moonshine
    upon the Couch.
Ber. Nay, never pull, for I will not go.
Lov. Then you must be carryed. [*carrying her.*]
Ber. [*Very softly*] Help, help, I'm Ravish'd, ruin'd, undone. O Lord, I
    shall never be able to bear it.

Vanbrugh had very little originality and even this scene seems to
have been suggested by one in Crowne's *City Politiques* (II.i) where
Lucinda behaves to Artall in much the same way:

Luc. I am betrayed! drawn into a snare! [*Aside*] But 'tis a sweet one—
    Help, help, help!
Art. I need no help, my dear.
Luc. But I do. Help, help! [*Aside*] Oh, 'tis a lovely gentleman!—Help,
    help! [*Aside*] 'tis a delicate gentleman!—Help, help!
Art. Why do you call so loud? I can help you to what you want.
Luc. Help, help! Will you force me? [*Aside*] I can't resist him—Help
    help!

Vanbrugh is less successful with the scenes depicting the virtuous
Amanda and her erring husband. This is partly because he chose to
write them in verse, following Cibber's example, without the
imagination, the technique or even the ear which the medium
demanded. The scenes are not deliberately mawkish, and they are
not intended, as far as one can tell, as a kind of parody of Cibber's,
as Loveless shows no signs of relapsing until Act II. Worthy is much
more credible, though more interesting when he is plotting with
Berinthia than when he is converted by Amanda and indulging in
unacknowledged pentameters:

> The Coarser Appetite of Nature's gone,
> and 'tis, methinks, the Food of Angels I require;
> how long this influence may last, Heaven knows.
> But in this moment of my purity,
> I cou'd on her own terms accept her Heart.
> Yes, lovely Woman, I can accept it.
> For now 'tis doubly worth my Care.
> Your charms are much encreas'd, since thus adorn'd.
> When Truth's extorted from us, then we own
> the Robe of Vertue is a graceful Habit.

The most original part of the play is to be found in the country
scenes. The nurse and Miss Hoyden may owe something to Miss
Prue and her nurse, but the atmosphere of Clumsey's household,
though more proper to farce than comedy, is Vanbrugh's own, from
the words with which young Fashion is received: 'Tummus, is the
blunderbuss prim'd?'.

Vanbrugh's aim in writing, as he confessed, was not to reform the
manners or morals of the age, but to amuse gentlemen of the town
and 'to divert (if possible) some part of their Spleen, in spite of their
Wives and their Taxes'. Despite this admission, it could be argued
that Vanbrugh was quite serious in his criticism of literary sentimentality and humbug, as in his next play, as we shall see, he was
making valid criticisms of *marriage à la mode*.

The Provok'd Wife, though generally regarded as Vanbrugh's best play, deals with traditional situations; its characters are long-established types; and its dialogue, though mostly quite natural,[1] lacks wit and sparkle. We have the boorish husband who no longer loves his young and beautiful wife; the wife who thinks of accepting as a lover the man who has loved her for years, and her niece whose suitor had vowed never to marry. Even Lady Fancyfull is similar to many affected ladies in other Restoration plays. Only her French maid and Sir John Brute's valet, Rasor, have more originality. Hazlitt spoke enthusiastically of the scene between Rasor and Mademoiselle—'than which nothing was ever more happily conceived, or done to more absolute perfection'—but one suspects that he was remembering a particularly good performance, rather than the text itself. Mademoiselle gives a description of the scene between Constant and Lady Brute, which had in fact been interrupted before the point described by Mademoiselle, and Rasor stands in for Constant:

> He tak her by the Hand: She turn her Head one oder Way. Den he squeez very hard; . . . Den she give him, Leetel pat. Den he Kiss her Tettons. Den she say—Pish, nay fee. Den he tremble, Den she— Sigh. Den he pull her into de Arbour: Den she pinch him.
> *Rasor* Aye, but not so hard, you Baggage, you.

Sir John Brute is not merely a boorish sot: he engages in murderous outrages with Lord Rake, and he is too much of a coward to fight when he thinks himself cuckolded. His most amusing scenes are those in which he attacks the watch dressed in a clergyman's gown and is brought before a puzzled magistrate. But, with the passage of time, these scenes were thought to be attacks on religion, or at least on the Church, and Vanbrugh in 1725 rewrote them. Instead of putting on a clerical gown, Sir John is made to disguise himself in one of his wife's dresses. The revised version is more farcical, because of the transvestism, but it contains some amusing satire of a day in the life of a woman of fashion.[2]

It is not quite fair to Vanbrugh to say that all his characters and

---

[1] In IV.4 Lady Brute and Constant rise into Vanbrugh's unacknowledged and undistinguished verse. See the seven speeches beginning 'Your glass and conscience will inform you, Madam'. Horace Walpole, however (op. cit., p. 315), says that Vanbrugh is 'the best writer of dialogue we have seen'.

[2] Garrick apparently disguised himself not as Lady Brute, but as a woman of the town, 'to suit the delicacy of the town', as one critic oddly explains. His acting in this part was said to be irresistible.

situations are stereotyped. Constant has loved Lady Brute for two years ever since her wedding day and his passion is unrequited, or at least unconsummated, when the curtain falls. His constancy marks him off from most heroes of Restoration comedy, as Lady Brute's procrastination marks her off from most of her sex as the dramatists saw them. What makes Lady Brute a sympathetic character is not merely the treatment she receives from her husband, but her occasional strokes of wit (as when she turns off a biblical text by saying 'That may be a mistake in the Translation') and still more by her realisation that it is wrong to arouse passions one has no intention of gratifying:

> So you see I'm no Coquet, *Bellinda*: And if you'll follow my advice, you'll never be one neither. 'Tis true, Coquettry is one of the main ingredients in the natural Composition of a Woman; and I as well as others, cou'd be well enough pleas'd to see a Crowd of young Fellows Ogling, and Glancing, and Watching all occasions to do forty foolish officious things: Nay . . . if I shou'd let pure Woman alone, I should e'en be but too well pleas'd with it.
>
> *Bel.* I'll swear 'twould tickle me strangely.
>
> *Lady Brute* But, after all, 'tis a Vicious practice in us, to give the least encouragement but where we design to come to a Conclusion. For 'tis an unreasonable thing to engage a Man in a Disease, which we beforehand resolve we never will apply a Cure to.

Although Sir John's complaint of the cloying sauce of matrimony is common form, we have to remember that Lady Brute married him for mercenary reasons and that he would not have married her if she had consented to be his lover. In the course of the play there are several discussions on marriage, the most serious of which is between Heartfree and Constant in the last act (V.2). Heartfree has previously appeared in the rôle of a critic of the female sex, both in his savage attack on Lady Fanciful's affectations and in the conversation with Constant later in the same scene. He boasts there that he has avoided falling in love by a rational analysis of women:

> I always consider a Woman, not as the Taylor, the Shoo-maker, the Tire-woman, the Sempstress, and (which is more than all that), the Poet makes her; but I consider her as pure Nature has contriv'd her, and that more strictly than I shou'd have done our old Grand-mother *Eve*, had I seen her naked in the Garden; for I consider her turn'd inside out. Her Heart well examin'd, I find there Pride, Vanity, Covetousness, Indiscretion; but, above all things, Malice; Plots eternally forging to destroy one—another's Reputations, and as

honestly to charge the Levity of Mens Tongues with the Scandal;
hourly Debates how to make poor Gentlemen in love with 'em, with
no other intent but to use 'm like Dogs when they have done; a
constant Desire of doing more mischief and an everlasting War
waged against Truth and Good-nature.

This misogynistic diatribe is undercut in advance by what we have
seen of Lady Brute and Bellinda; and Heartfree, when he falls in
love, is reluctantly compelled to retract. In Act V he begins by
telling Constant that the 'matrimonial remedy' is worse than the
disease; and says: 'I may reasonably be allowed to boggle at
marrying the niece, in the very moment that you are debauching
the aunt'. But a minute later he confesses that 'the wife seldom
rambles, till the husband shows her the way' and that he would
never fear that Bellinda would cuckold him. He no longer blames
female frailty but the inconstancy of men, 'the very charge we so
impudently throw upon (indeed) a steadier and more generous sex'.
Not unnaturally, Constant expresses surprise that Heartfree should
grow so warm an advocate for women, and he tells him:

> Why, 'faith, *Heartfree*, Matrimony is like an Army going to engage.
> Love's the forlorn Hope, which is soon cut off; the Marriage-Knot
> is the main Body, which may stand Buff a long, long time; and
> Repentance is the Rear-Guard, which rarely gives ground as long as
> the main Battle has a Being.

Heartfree takes this not very perspicuous image to mean that
Constant advises him 'to whore on, as you do'. There follows the
significant passage of dialogue:

Const. That's not concluded yet. For tho' Marriage be a Lottery, in
which there are a wondrous many Blanks, yet there is one inestimable
Lot, in which the only Heaven on Earth is written. Wou'd your kind
Fate but guide your Hand to that, tho' I were wrapt in all that
Luxury itself could cloath me with, I still shou'd envy you.

Heart. And justly too; For to be capable of loving one, doubtless is better
than to possess a Thousand. But how far that Capacity's in me,
alas! I know not.

Vanbrugh, as so often in sententious passages, has dropped into
the rhythms of blank verse. But there is no doubt that this is one of
the two morals of the play. The other is expressed by Southerne's
title, *The Wives' Excuse: or Cuckolds make Themselves.* Constant,
indeed, makes the same point:

"Tis true, a man of real worth scarce ever is a cuckold, but by his own fault'.[1]

Vanbrugh's next plays were adaptations—*Aesop* (1697) from the French of Boursault; *The Pilgrim* from Fletcher's comedy (1700); *The False Friend* from the French of La Sage, with some use of the Spanish original (1702); and *The Confederacy* from Dancourt's *Les Bourgeoises à la Mode* (1705).

Vanbrugh's adaptation of *Les Bourgeoises à la Mode* was deservedly popular. Dancourt's play was first performed in 1692; and *The Confederacy* at the end of October 1705. Vanbrugh's first scene between Mrs Amlet and Mrs Cloggit was his own invention, and it was designed to reveal to the audience—before his first appearance—that Dick is posing as a gentleman and living on his wits. Dancourt, on the other hand, reveals the relationship between Dick and his mother only when they meet later. Vanbrugh rightly judged that it was better to prepare the audience. The first scene of Act II in which Dick tells his mother that he hopes to marry Corinna and so buys her silence is also Vanbrugh's addition: Mrs Amlet's mingling of reproach and affection is one of the best things in the play. In the same scene Dick steals the necklace in sight of the audience, whereas in Dancourt's play we hear of the disappearance of the necklace only when Madame Amelin comes to see Lisette in III.3. Vanbrugh adds a brief scene between Brass and Flippanta at the beginning of Act V and another brief scene before the entrance of Mr Clip in V.2. He also omits several passages (e.g. IV.3, V.6.) from Dancourt's play.

What is more significant than these alterations is the additional flavour Vanbrugh gives to the dialogue. Dancourt's is not particularly memorable. Lisette's soliloquy at the end of Act I is made much more racy in Flippanta's corresponding speech:

> Adieu, Madame Amelin. Nous aurons donc de l'argent comptant, et nous donnerons à jouer, Dieu merci. Tout se dispose à merveilles pour ma petite fortune. La passion du Chevalier, l'humeur de ma Maitresse, qui ne songe qu'à ruiner son mari: elle achète cher, vend à bon marché, met tout en gage; Je suis son Intendante. Voilà comme les Maitresses deviennent Soubrettes, et comme les Soubrettes deviennent quelque fois Maitresses à leur tour.

---

[1] Bernard Harris, *Sir John Vanbrugh* (1967), p. 27, says that the play 'concludes in mutual pardon and acknowledgement of faults'. This applies to Heartfree and Bellinda, but not to the Brutes.

Adieu, Mrs Amlet. So—this ready Money will make us all happy.
This Spring will set our Basset going, and that's a Wheel will turn
Twenty others. My Lady's young and handsome; she'll have a Dozen
Intrigues upon her Hands, before she has been Twice at her Prayers.
So much the better; the more the Grist, the richer the Miller. Sure
never Wench got into so hopeful a Place: Here's a Fortune to be
Sold, a Mistress to be debauch'd, and a Master to be ruin'd. If I
don't feather my Nest and get a good Husband, I deserve to die,
both a maid and a beggar.

In Act II, referring to her lover's letter, Mariane merely says:
'Il écrit comme ses yeux parlent, ils m'avoient déja dit tout ce qui
est dans sa lettre'. But Corinna provides the audience with extracts
and a nice comment:

> Let me read it, let me read it, let me read it, let me read it, I say. Um,
> um, um *Cupid's*, um, um, um, *Darts*, um, um, um, *Beauty*, um,
> *Charms*, um, um, um, *Angel*, um, *Goddess*, um—[*kissing the letter*],
> um, um, um, *truest Lover*, hum, um, *Eternal Constancy*, um, um,
> um, *cruel*, um, um, um, *Racks*, um, um, *Tortures*, um, um, *Fifty
> Daggers*, um, um, *bleeding Heart*, um, um, *dead Man*. Very well, a
> mighty civil Letter, I promise you; not one smutty Word in it: I'll
> go lock it up in my Comb-box.

Mariane is a colourless *ingénue*; Corinna is given some individuality.
  Later in the same scene, Flippanta, unlike Lisette, is given a
snatch of song; and whereas M. Simon expresses surprise that his
wife has already left the house—'à l'heure qu'il est, elle n'est pas
eveillée le plus souvent'—Gripe is more vivid:

> Why, she uses to be stewing in her bed three hours after this time, as
> late a 'tis.

Or again, Flippanta's soliloquy, at the end of the act, adds life and
vigour to Lisette's brief comment:

> Ah! que les pauvres maris sont bient nés pour être dupes! Il va
> quereller sa femme pour lui faire faire une chose qu'elle souhaite,
> et dont il aura peut-être plus à enrager que de tout ce qu'elle a
> jamais pu faire.

> Nay, thou hast a blessed time on't, that must be confess'd. What a
> miserable Devil is a Husband! Insupportable to himself, and a
> Plague to everything about them. Their Wives do by them, as Children
> do by Dogs, teaze and provoke 'em, 'till they make them so curs'd,

they snarl and bite at everything that comes in their reach. This
Wretch here is grown perverse to that degree, he's for his Wife's
keeping home, and making Hell of his House, so he may be the
Devil in it, to torment her. How niggardly soever he is, of all things
he possesses, he is willing to purchase her Misery, at the expence of
his own Peace. But he'd as good be still, for he'll miss of his Aim. If
I know her (which I think I do) she'll set his Blood in such a Ferment,
it shall bubble out at every Pore of him; whilst hers is so quiet in her
Veins, her Pulse shall go like a Pendulum.

It is not surprising that Mrs Bracegirdle made a great hit in the part.
A final comparison may be made between the scene in which
Brass blackmails Dick into promising him the diamond necklace,
merely by raising his voice and terrifying Dick that someone will
hear, with the corresponding scene in Dancourt:

Frontin Point, Monsieur; il y a encore ce diamant que vous avez
    tantôt pris chez votre mère, et que vous m'avez dit de troquer contre
    de l'argent.
Le Chevalier Ah! Frontin.
Frontin Ah! Monsieur, point de contestations, s'il vous plait; je n'aime
    point qu'on me contredise, moi.
Le Chevalier J'enrage! Hé bien! le diamant te demeura; feras-tu content?

Brass It is not indeed. There's a Diamond Necklace you robb'd your
    Mother of ev'n now.
Dick Ah, you *Jew*.
Brass No Words.
Dick My dear *Brass*!
Brass I insist.
Dick My old Friend.
Brass [*raising his voice*] Dick Amlet, I insist.
Dick Ah the Cormorant—well, 'tis thine: But thou'lt never thrive by it.
Brass When I find it begins to do me Mischief, I'll give it you again.

The Confederacy deals with middle-class life and in its milieu and
style it is closer to Jacobean Citizen Comedy than to the comedy of
manners. Dick Amlet is regarded as a suitable match for Corinna,
despite his false pretences, as soon as it is revealed that he will have
money from his mother. Dancourt's skilled plotting is united to
Vanbrugh's natural dialogue to make what is probably his most
successful play. As Hazlitt said, it is 'a comedy of infinite contrivance
and intrigue, with a matchless spirit of impudence'.
When Vanbrugh died in 1726 he left an unfinished play, *A Journey*

to London. There are three and a half acts in the fragment, but as the
scenes are not properly linked together it seems probable that
Vanbrugh intended to write additional scenes for the completed
acts. The individual scenes are as good as anything he ever wrote,
with lively dialogue and excellent characterisation; but it looks as
though Vanbrugh failed to complete the play because he had not
worked out a satisfactory plot. The initial situation is admirable: Sir
Francis Headpiece, a newly elected M.P., arrives in London with his
family. The caustic comments of Uncle Richard about the foolishness
of Sir Francis in consulting his wife, and getting elected; the bustle
and confusion about the family's arrival; the overturning of their
new coach which they can ill afford—all these are conveyed brilliantly. 'Forty years and two is the Age of him', says Uncle Richard,

> in which it is computed by his Butler, his own person has drank two
> and thirty Ton of Ale. The rest of his Time has been employ'd in
> persecuting all the poor four-legged creatures round, that wou'd
> but run away fast enough from him, to give him the high-mettled
> pleasure of running after them. In this noble Employ, he has broke
> his right Arm, his left Leg, and both his Collar-bones—once he broke
> his Neck, but that did him no harm; a nimble Hedge-leaper, a
> Brother of the Stirrup that was by, whipt off his Horse and mended it.

The scene between Lord Loverule and his wife in Act II is quite the
best matrimonial quarrel in all Vanbrugh's works; and Lady
Arabella's account to Clarinda of the pleasures of conversation
between husband and wife has a sparkle Vanbrugh seldom achieved
elsewhere.

Clar. . . . surely it must be mighty agreeable when a Man and his Wife
    can give themselves the same turn of Conversation.
Lady Arm. O, the prettiest Thing in the World.
Clar. But yet, tho' I believe there's no Life so happy as a marry'd one, in
    the main; yet I fansy, where two people are so very much together,
    they must often be in want of something to talk upon.
Lady Ara. Clarinda, you are the most mistaken in the world; marry'd
    People have things to talk of, Child, that never enter into the Imagina-
    tion of others. Why now, here's my Lord and I, we han't been
    marry'd above two short Years you know, and we have already
    eight or ten Things constantly in Bank, that whenever we want
    Company, we can talk of any one of them for two Hours together,
    and the Subject never the flatter. It will be as fresh next Day, if we
    have occasion for it, as it was the first day it entertain'd us.
Clar. Why, that must be wonderful pretty.

Lady Ara. O, there's no life like it.

This dialogue comes just after we have witnessed Lady Arabella quarrelling with her husband because he goes to bed early and she goes to bed late, a subject which they have obviously discussed many times before.

Vanbrugh has had enthusiastic admirers. Horace Walpole thought[1] his plays were superior to Congreve's:

It is the proof of consummate art in a comic writer, when you seem to have passed your time at the theatre as you might have done out of it—it proves he has exactly hit the style, manners, and character of his contemporaries.

But is must be admitted that Vanbrugh suffers by comparison with other Restoration dramatists. He was less original than Wycherley, Congreve, or even Farquhar and his dialogue lacks the wit and polish of Congreve's, the force of Wycherley's, the humour of Farquhar's last two plays. As an architect, Vanbrugh was a professional: as a dramatist, he was an amateur.

[1] op. cit., p. 316.

9

GEORGE FARQUHAR

Farquhar was born in Londonderry in 1677, the son of a clergyman. He entered Trinity College, Dublin, in 1694 and left two years later. From a remark in his first play—'We dare not have wit there, for fear of being counted rakes'—it has been deduced that there is some truth in the rumour that he was expelled for profanity. But there is no official record of his expulsion, and it is perhaps more likely that Farquhar left of his own accord, attracted by the thought of a theatrical career. After some experience as an actor in Dublin, he came to London with Robert Wilks, who was later to shine in the part of Sir Harry Wildair.

Love and a Bottle, Farquhar's first and feeblest comedy, was performed in 1698. There is nothing of interest in either the plot or the characters; and the Irish hero, Roebuck, fornicator and drunkard, is apparently regarded by the author as a man whose virtues, which are not very apparent, outweigh his vices, and not as an object of satire. The only sign that Farquhar might develop into a tolerable dramatist is an occasional liveliness in the dialogue.

The Constant Couple, Farquhar's second play, is a very great improvement. It has some brisk scenes and one well-drawn character, Sir Harry Wildair. This was a favourite acting part, sometimes played by women, and the chief reason for the continued popularity of the play. But in other respects the play is seriously defective. The main plot, which does not concern Sir Harry, depends on a double impossibility: that Lady Lurewell should not recognise the man who had seduced her some years before, and that Colonel Standard should not realise that the woman he now loves is the girl he once seduced. Nor does Lady Lurewell's conduct in the course of the play, avenging the wrongs of her sex on her would-be lovers, make a happy ending either plausible or satisfying. The other plot is also badly constructed. In the second scene of Act II Sir Harry meets Clincher Junior at Angelica's house. In the third scene of Act III, after he has talked with Standard, visited Lady Lurewell's, and met Clincher's elder brother, Sir Harry returns to Angelica's house to find that time has stood still during his absence: Clincher Junior is still in process of being introduced to Angelica.

The other great defect of the play is that at moments Farquhar adopts an inflated diction and falls into the rhythms of blank verse, as in Angelica's speech in the first scene of Act V:

> What madness, *Sir Harry*, what wild Dream of loose Desire could prompt you to attempt this Baseness? View me well.—The Brightness of my Mind, methinks, should lighten outwards, and let you see your Mistake in my Behaviour. I think it shines with so much Innocence in my Face, that it should dazzle all your vicious Thoughts. Think not I am defenceless 'cause alone. Your very self is Guard against yourself: I'm sure there's something generous in your Soul; My Words shall search it out, and Eyes shall fire it for my own Defence.

Sir Harry accuses her of having come from reading Nat Lee and says she is the first whore in heroics he has met with. But she is not the only heroine of the period who protests too much. One of the faults of sentimental comedy is that its characters are apt to be self-conscious about their virtues, as though they were spiritual *nouveaux riches*. Farquhar suffered also from the fact that he was a very poor poet. Yet the scenes between Sir Harry and Angelica are the best in the play. They embody a genuinely comic situation. Vizard, who has been repulsed by Angelica, has his revenge by telling Sir Harry she is a prostitute, and (in his letter of introduction) telling her mother Sir Harry is a suitor for Angelica's hand. Sir Harry and Angelica are therefore talking all the time at cross-purposes, Sir Harry supposing that she is offended when he offers her money only because he has not offered her enough.

The play has plenty of bustling action, some of it farcical. The elder Clincher's gaiety is explained by the fact that he is in mourning for his father and, later in the play, the younger Clincher is delighted to hear of his brother's death and even gets Tom Errand to swear that he has killed him. This sort of insensibility is proper to farce, but not to comedy. Yet Farquhar is not without touches of wit. He has some neat satire of the reformation of the stage by Jeremy Collier:

We are all so reformed that gallantry is taken for vice, and hypocrisy for religion.

In the last act, Alderman Smuggler, who is a swindler and a hypocrite, says:

> Lord! Lord! What Business has a Prentice at a Playhouse, unless it be to hear his Master made a Cuckold, and his Mistriss a Whore! 'Tis ten to one now, but some malicious Poet has my Character upon the Stage within this *Month*: 'Tis a hard matter now, that an honest sober *Man* can't Sin in private for this Plaguy Stage. I gave an honest Gentleman Five Guineas myself towards Writing a Book against it: And it has done no good, we see.

Sometimes, however, the satire is turned, not against the citizen, but against the gentleman. When Mrs Errand discovers Clincher in her husband's clothes, she accuses him: 'Oh, Mr. Constable, here's a rogue that has murdered my husband, and robbed him of his clothes'. At which the Constable exclaims: 'Murder and robbery! then he must be a gentleman'.

Farquhar's next play, *Sir Harry Wildair*, was a sequel to *The Constant Couple*, and generally inferior to it. It has a wretched plot—Sir Harry's wife, supposed dead, disguises herself as a ghost, and Colonel Standard's wife nearly commits adultery—but there are some amusing passages of dialogue. One of these is Parly's confession to Standard of her methods of obtaining money. The other is Sir Harry's discourse on honour in the last act:

> Look ye, my Lord, when you and I were under the Tuition of our Governors, and convers'd only with old *Cicero, Livy, Virgil, Plutarch*, and the like; why, then such a Man was a Villain, and such a one was a Man of Honour: but now that I have known the Court, a little of what they call the *Beau-monde* and the *Belle-esprit*, I find that Honour looks as ridiculous as *Roman* Buskins upon your Lordship, or my full Peruke upon *Scipio Africanus* . . . Because the World's improved, my Lord, and we find that this Honour is a very troublesom and impertinent Thing. Can't we live together like good Neighbours and Christians, as they do in *France*? I lend you my Coach, I borrow yours; you Dine with me, I Sup with you; I lie with your Wife, and you lie with mine.—Honour! That's such an Impertinence!—Pray, my Lord, hear me. What does your Honour think of murdering your Friend's Reputation? making a Jest of his Misfortunes? cheating him at Cards, debauching his Bed, or the like?

Lord Bellamy exlaims: 'Why, rank Villainy'; and Sir Harry retorts:

> Pish! pish! nothing but good Manners, excess of good Manners.
> Why, you han't been at Court lately.

Farquhar's next play, *The Twin Rivals* (1702), is not really a
comedy of manners. In the preface he claims that he has learnt
from Collier's strictures on the immorality of contemporary drama
and that he has 'endeavoured to show, that an English comedy may
answer the strictness of poetical justice' by punishing the immoral
characters at the end of the play. But, he says, the audience were
disappointed; for, as one of them said: 'however pious we may
appear at home, yet we never go to that end of the town but with
an intention to be lewd'.

Farquhar thought that the most material objection to the play
was that the vices of some of the characters were examples of
wickedness—'a middle sort of wickedness'—rather than folly; but
he argued that, as the characters were too mean for tragedy, 'they
must of necessity drop into comedy'. This is true enough; but the
trouble about the play is that it contains hardly any wit or humour,
and very little satire. The situations, and much of the language,
belong to sentimental comedy. The chief interest—the only interest,
indeed—is to see what happens next, in particular to see how the
plots of the villains will be frustrated. Benjamin Wouldbe plots with
a midwife and a scoundrelly lawyer to succeed to his father's estate
and so disinherit his virtuous elder brother, Hermes; and Richmore
plots to marry his pregnant mistress to his unsuspecting nephew,
Trueman, and to rape Aurelia. The plots are linked by the fact that
Aurelia is a friend of Constance, beloved by the twin brothers, and
also by the fact that Mandrake is a bawd as well as a midwife.
Aurelia is rescued in the nick of time by Trueman; Richmore
promises to marry the woman he has seduced—though in the preface
Farquhar declares that after the fall of the curtain he changes his
mind; Benjamin is foiled when Mrs Mandrake is compelled to
confess, and Hermes marries Constance.

The sentimentality may be seen at its worst in the scene (III.3)
where Hermes enters Constance's room unperceived to find her in
tears, because she thinks he is dead.

Hermes In Tears! perhaps for me! I'll try.
 [*Drops a Picture, and goes back to the entrance, and listens.*]
Aurelia If there be aught in Grief delightful, don't grudge me a share.
F

Constance No, my dear *Aurelia*, I'll ingross it all. I lov'd him so, methinks
   I should be jealous if any mourned his death besides myself. What's
   here?—[*Takes up the Picture.*] Ha! see, Cousin—the very Face and
   Features of the Man! Sure, some officious Angel had brought me
   this for a Companion in my Solitude! Now I'm fitted out for Sorrow!
   With this I'll sigh, with this converse, gaze on his Image till I grow
   blind with weeping!
Aurelia I'm amazed! how came it here?
Constance Whether by Miracle or humane Chance, 'tis all alike; I have
   it here. Nor shall it ever separate from my Breast. It is the only thing
   cou'd give me joy; because it will increase my Grief.
Hermes [*Coming forward*] Most Glorious Woman! Now I am fond of
   life.

The mawkishness of the sentiments, the tendency to drop into poetic
diction and verse rhythms, show Farquhar at his worst. The play
deserved to fail; and its failure proved salutary to the dramatist for
it led him to seek for a new form of comedy which would avoid
both the sentimentality of his last play and the 'manners' formula
which was already wearing thin. Vanbrugh in *The Relapse* had
already set some scenes outside London; and Farquhar's experiences
as a recruiting officer in Lichfield and Shrewsbury suggested the
theme of one of his remaining plays and the settings of both.

   Farquhar has been praised by some critics, notably Archer and
Strauss, for breaking away from London and showing us[1]

the life of the inn, the market-place, and the manor house. He showed us
the squire, the justice, the innkeeper, the highwayman, the recruiting
sergeant, the charitable lady, the country belle, the chambermaid, and
half a score of excellent rustic types . . . Farquhar reduced wit within
something like the limits of nature, subordinating it to humour, and giving
it, at the same time, an accent, all his own, of unforced, buoyant gaiety.

Other critics, who lament the decline of the comedy of manners,
are inclined to blame Farquhar for substituting sentiment and
humour for wit and satire. *The Twin Rivals* may justly be deplored;
but Farquhar deserves the credit of learning from his mistake and
of discovering a new vein of comedy after the old one was exhausted.
Not only was there a changed climate of opinion, but also a move
by the Lord Chamberlain against profanity and indecency. Farquhar
himself, or his publisher, deleted from the second edition of *The
Recruiting Officer* two passages which had appeared in the first.

[1] William Archer's introduction (1906), p. 24, and cf. Louis A. Strauss, ed. *The
Recruiting Officer and The Beaux' Stratagem* (1914), Introduction.

In Act IV Silvia had asked Plume—in French—if he had slept with Rose; and Act V had begun with a scene in which Rose sulked because she had not been seduced, as she had hoped.

The Recruiting Officer and *The Beaux' Stratagem* are Farquhar's most original plays and greatly superior to anything he had written before. They both have excellent plots, amusing characters, and lively dialogue; and they both kept their popularity on the boards during the whole of the eighteenth century and after. Indeed, two of the most notable revivals in the present century were that of *The Beaux' Stratagem* by Nigel Playfair at Hammersmith, with Edith Evans as Mrs Sullen (1927), and the National Theatre production of *The Recruiting Officer* in 1963.

The Recruiting Officer was first performed on 8 April 1706 and it was an immediate success. It had been written so hastily that there are several inconsistencies.[1] Lucy forges Melinda's name and yet, later, steals her signature. Silvia calls herself Jack Wilful and Captain Pinch in different scenes without anyone commenting on the discrepancy. In III.2 Plume quotes two couplets previously used by Brazen though Plume had not overheard him. But it is unlikely that these points would be noticed during a performance of the play.

The scenes which give the play its title are concerned with recruiting, and the rivalry to obtain recruits between Plume and Brazen. This ends with Plume disposing of his recruits to Brazen when he himself is to 'raise recruits the matrimonial way'. The second plot is concerned with Silvia's disguising herself as a man for love of Plume; and in the end she wins his hand. The third plot concerns Worthy's love for the heiress Melinda and his jealousy of Brazen because of Lucy's tricks. The three plots are linked together in various ways. Melinda's quarrel with Silvia leads her to write the letter which makes Balance forbid his daughter to think of Plume for a husband, and this makes Silvia disguise herself. Both Brazen and Plume attempt to enlist her; and Brazen is Plume's rival as a recruiting officer and Worthy's rival in love. Melinda and Lucy, as well as potential recruits, visit Kite when he sets up as a fortune-teller. Balance as Justice of the Peace decides which men shall be recruited.

Plume, the nominal hero of the play, is an amiable rake, who will presumably turn over a new leaf when he is married to Silvia. This, at least, is the implication of Balance's speech to Worthy (III.1):

[1] cf. Robert L. Hough's articles in *N.Q.* (August 1953, November 1954).

> I was just such another Fellow at his Age. I never set my Heart upon
> any Woman so much as to make my self uneasie at the Disappoint-
> ment. But what was very surprizing both to myself and Friends, I
> chang'd o' th' sudden from the most fickle Lover to be the most
> constant Husband in the World.

There is, of course, an element of sentimentality in this attitude;
and elsewhere Farquhar feels it necessary to explain that, despite
his bastards, Plume is not as bad as his reputation. He tells the
disguised Silvia:

> No, Faith, I'm not that Rake that the World imagines; I have got an
> Air of Freedom, which People mistake for Lewdness in me, as they
> mistake Formality in others for Religion.—The World is all a Cheat;
> only I take mine, which is undesign'd, to be more excusable than
> theirs, which is hypocritical. I hurt no body but my self, and they
> abuse all Mankind—Will you lye with me?

The last five words of this speech are presumably not intended by
Plume in a sexual sense; but as he has already kissed 'Jack Wilfull'
and admitted 'his' charm, the spectator is bound to regard the words
as equivocal.

Melinda tells Silvia that if she had been a man she would have
'been the greatest Rake in *Christendom*'; and Silvia confesses:

> I should have endeavour'd to know the World, which a Man can
> never do thoroughly without half a hundred Friendships, and as
> many Amours.

In accordance with this view, she agrees to be godfather to Plume's
bastard, and she arranges to sleep with Rose, to protect her from
Plume, rather than out of jealousy. In her masculine attire, she
apes the manners and language of rakes, so that through her
Farquhar is able to satirise what he partly admires.

More interesting than either hero or heroine are the comic rogues,
Sergeant Kite and Captain Brazen. Some of Kite's illegal methods
of recruiting are reminiscent of those used by Falstaff in *Henry IV*.
But, in addition, he gets some of his recruits by disguising himself
as a fortune-teller; he goes through a form of marriage with Plume's
cast-off mistresses; and, despite his roguery, he endears himself to
the audience by his ingenuity and by the effrontery of his auto-
biography:

You must know, Sir, I was born a Gypsie, and bred among that Crew till I was ten Year old; there I learn'd Canting and Lying. I was brought from my Mother, *Cleopatra*, by a certain Nobleman for three Pistols, who, liking my Beauty, made me his Page; there I learned Impudence and Pimping; I was turn'd off for wearing my Lord's Linen, and drinking my Lady's Brandy, and then turn'd Bailiff's Follower. There I learn'd Bullying and Swearing. I at last got into the Army, and there I learn'd Whoring and Drinking—So that if you Worship pleases to cast up the whole Sum, *viz.*, Canting, Lying, Impudence, Pimping, Bullying, Swearing, Whoring, Drinking and a Halbard, you will find the Sum Total will amount to a Recruiting Sergeant.

Brazen is an equally effective stage character—and a favourite rôle of actors—but his lies and affectations and the exaggeration with which Farquhar depicts them make him a figure of farce. Rose and the recruits are nicely sketched in and the only unsatisfactory characters in the play are Worthy and Melinda. Worthy is dull and acts only as a foil to Plume; Melinda is likewise a foil to Silvia and her actions are determined by the necessities of the plot.

There is very little wit in the dialogue—perhaps Farquhar felt that the comedy of wit had reached its apotheosis in Congreve—but there is plenty of humour, which British audiences have always found more to their taste. When, for example, Kite translates 'Carolus' on a coin as Queen Anne; or when the Constable introduces the three Justices and himself as 'four very honest gentlemen'; or when the Justices enlist a man because his wife has a child each year and the wife says, 'Look'e Mr Captain, the parish shall get nothing by sending him away; for I won't lose my teeming time if there be a man left in the parish'; or when Rose, disappointed with her bedfellow, complains to Silvia, 'I wonder you could have the conscience to ruin a poor girl for nothing'—such remarks reveal Farquhar as an admirable writer of comedy, but of a comedy far removed from that of the fashionable drawing-room. *The Recruiting Officer* is completely free from the sentimentality of the previous plays. This may be due to the fact that Farquhar knew more about recruiting than he did about fashionable society.

The laughter which the play provokes as M. Hamard says,[1] is 'based on tolerance and the joyous acceptance of the world as it is—good in the eyes of the rational, sensible man'. Wit combats would be out of place in such a comedy.

The last of Farquhar's plays, written when he was dying, is also

[1] J. Hamard, *Le Ruse des Galants* (Paris, 1965), p. 91.

his best. *The Beaux' Stratagem* (1707) has a more original plot, a wittier dialogue, and a livelier group of characters than any of his previous plays. Some critics have complained that the comic Irish Jesuit, Foigard, is a comparative failure and that Count Bellair could be cut without great loss. As to Foigard, we may well agree; and the Bellair episode is a clumsy way of trying to arouse Sullen's jealousy. Another complaint which many critics have levelled against Farquhar is that the 'divorce' by mutual consent at the end of the play is too fantastic and farcical. To which one could argue that it is not intended to be realistic. The pretty ceremony is clearly Utopian. Farquhar had been studying Milton's plea for divorce on grounds other than adultery and he echoes several phrases from *The Doctrine and Discipline of Divorce*.[1] When Sullen tells his wife that they are 'two Carcasses join'd unnaturally together' and she retorts 'Or rather a living Soul coupled to a dead Body'; or when she asks if a bench can 'give Judgement upon Antipathies' and tells Dorinda that 'casual Violation is a transient Injury, and may possibly be repair'd' and that when there is a natural antipathy, 'not all the golden Links of Wedlock nor Iron Manacles of Law can keep 'em fast', Farquhar is paraphrasing or literally quoting from Milton's treatise. And when Mrs Sullen concludes Act III with some rhymed couplets—

> Must Man, the chiefest Work of Art Divine,
> Be doom'd in endless Discord to Repine?

we may be sure that the last word was suggested by Milton's account of the disappointed husband who 'sits repining'. It is reasonable to assume that the divorce scene, far from being farcical, was the thing with which Farquhar was deeply concerned. Mrs Sullen's predicament is pathetic and it could have been treated tragically. Married to a drunken boor, she has no escape under the actual laws at the beginning of the eighteenth century, and she is unwilling to adopt the usual recourse of ill-treated wives. She is allowed a number of complaints about the conduct of her husband, and in one or two places—e.g. the end of Act III or the beginning of Act IV—the comic muse is put to flight. But, in general, Farquhar makes her use her misfortunes as a subject for her wit, as in her splendid account of the pleasures of matrimony:

> O Sister, Sister! if ever you marry, beware of a sullen, silent Sot, one

[1] cf. M. A. Larson's article, *PMLA* (1924).

that's always musing, but never thinks:—There's some Diversion in
a talking Blockhead; and since a Woman must wear Chains; I wou'd
have the Pleasure of hearing 'em rattle a little. Now you shall see;
but take this by the way:—He came home this morning at his usual
Hour of Four, waken'd me out of a sweet Dream of something else,
by tumbling over the Tea-table, which he broke all to pieces; after
his Man and he had rowl'd about the Room, like sick Passengers in a
Storm, he comes flounce into Bed, dead as a Salmon into a Fish-
monger's basket; his Feet cold as Ice, his Breath hot as a Furnace,
and his Hands and his Face as greasy as his Flannel Night-cap.—
Oh Matrimony! He tosses up the Clothes with a barbarous swing
over his Shoulders, disorders the whole Œconomy of my Bed,
leaves me half naked, and my whole Night's Comfort is the tuneable
Serenade of that wakeful Nightingale, his Nose! O, the Pleasure of
counting the melancholly Clock by a snoring Husband!

Even if Squire Sullen had been a more amicable husband, it is
doubtful whether his wife would have been happy, for she shares
the opinions of most heroines of the comedy of manners about the
superiority of London life to that of the country. When Dorinda tells
her she shares in all the pleasures that the country affords, she
retorts:

Country Pleasures! Racks and Torments! Dost think, Child, that my
Limbs were made for leaping of Ditches, and clambring over Stiles?
or that my Parents, wisely foreseeing my future Happiness in Country
Pleasures, had early instructed me in the rural Accomplishments of
drinking fat Ale, playing at Whisk, and smoaking Tobacco with
my Husband?

Dorinda, Sullen's sister, is a rather colourless foil to his wife, and
she obtains as a husband the less interesting of the two adventurers.
Aimwell's conversion has been condemned as the intrusion of
sentimentality; but it is not so much the conversion as the language
in which it is expressed that is at fault:

Such goodness who cou'd injure! I find myself unequal to the Task
of Villain; she has gain'd my Soul, and made it honest like her own:
I cannot, cannot hurt her.

His confession that he is not Viscount Aimwell hardly deserves
Dorinda's exclamation: 'Matchless honesty!'

Archer, despite his unscrupulousness, is a gay and attractive
figure, whether he is making love to Cherry, making friends with

Scrub, trying to seduce Mrs Sullen, or fighting the robbers. Because he is posing as Aimwell's servant, he is able to move up and down the social scale and, being on the verge of penury, his conduct is treated by the author with leniency: for Farquhar himself, as he was writing the play, was dying in a garret.

A number of the minor characters are equally successful. Boniface, with his catch-phrase 'as the saying is', became the generic term for a country inn-keeper throughout the eighteenth century; Cherry, his daughter, has always been a favourite with audiences; Scrub, is a nice mixture of clown and simple-minded country servant; and Gibbet is an amusing rogue.

The dialogue of all these characters is sprightly and humorous. When Gibbet is asked to say a prayer before he is killed, he retorts: 'the government has provided a chaplain to say prayers for us on these occasions'. When Cherry says she is young and doesn't understand wheedling, Boniface exclaims:

> Young! why you Jade, as the saying is, can any Woman wheedle that is not young? Your Mother was useless at five and twenty. Not wheedle! would you make your Mother a Whore, and me a Cuckold, as the saying is?

Occasionally the play drops into farce as in the scene where Mrs Sullen, pretending to be her mother-in-law, advises a country-woman how to cure her husband's sore leg:

> Well, good Woman, I'll tell you what you must do. You must lay your Husband's Leg upon a table, and with a Chopping-knife you must lay it open as broad as you can; then you must take out the Bone and beat the Flesh soundly with a rowling-pin; then take Salt, Pepper, Cloves, Mace and Ginger, some sweet Herbs, and season it very well; then rowl it up like Brawn, and put it into the Oven for two Hours.

This is justified by its success. But, when Aimwell awakens from his bogus fit to declaim fustian, audiences tend to be embarrassed:

> Where am I?
> Sure I pass'd the Gulph of silent Death,
> And now I land on the *Elisian* Shore—
> Behold the Goddess of those happy Plains,
> Fair *Proserpine*—Let me adore thy bright Divinity.

In some respects the play looks forward to the novels of Fielding and Smollet; and in other respects it leads on to the comedies of Goldsmith. Farquhar is sometimes blamed for adulterating the comedy of manners; but he was writing for a different audience than the one which had witnessed *The Country Wife* a generation earlier. The old form of comedy was in decline and Farquhar was right to seek for a new form as well as a different subject-matter.

But Farquhar's most staunch admirer, William Archer, praises him for largely irrelevant reasons; that he has a 'sweeter, cleaner, healthier mind' than Congreve or Wycherley; that his characters are less repulsive; that he is more humane than his contemporaries; that his dialogue is more natural because he is not, like Congreve, always striving to be witty; that he gets on with the plot and does not engage in irrelevant discussions; and that he admitted a moral standard.[1]

To all this one may retort that, from the moral point of view, Aimwell's desire to marry a wealthy heiress by pretending to be a lord is worse than any action of Valentine or Mirabell; and the actions of Aimwell and Archer are not rendered more moral by the former's repentance or the latter's failure. Some of Farquhar's dialogue is natural enough; but in many passages he is guilty of pseudo-poetic rant, much further from natural speech than anything in Congreve. Dialogue should not be a mere reproduction of everyday speech and, of course, characters in a play should not be assessed by their virtuousness or wickedness, or we should be in danger of supposing that Falstaff and Volpone were inferior to the Good-Natured Man.

---

[1] W. Archer, Introduction to Mermaid, ed., pp. 15–29.

I O

DECLINE AND RENEWAL

The history of drama in the eighteenth century makes depressing reading. It shows the unavailing efforts of a handful of writers to break the stranglehold of sentimentality. If moral literature is that which gives a true picture of life, and immoral literature that which gives a false picture, we are bound to conclude that sentimental comedy is comparatively immoral, and the comedy of Wycherley and Congreve comparatively moral. Yet the sentimentalists believed their plays would have a beneficial effect on the morals of audiences, who duly approved—even if they were not improved.

Richard Steele, a professed admirer of Collier, wrote *The Lying Lover* (1703) 'to banish out of conversation all entertainment which does not proceed from simplicity of mind, good nature, friendship and honour'. His ambition was 'to attempt a comedy which might be no improper entertainment in a Christian Commonwealth'. The play was nevertheless 'damned for its piety'. In *The Tender Husband* (1705) Steele again tried to be 'very careful to avoid everything that might look ill-natured, immoral, or prejudicial to what the better part of mankind hold sacred and honourable'. *The Conscious Lovers* (1722), Steele's most successful play, was designed to attack duelling. One can respect his intentions in all his plays—even if one suspects an element of calculation and a desire to be in the swim—but the results are disastrous. Steele, as we know from his essays, had a delightful sense of humour, but his moralistic purpose in his comedies seems to have inhibited it. His dialogue had come to be far removed from the language of real life; there is little wit, or even fun, in his plays; and the characters are dummies.

Whereas the classical conception of comedy is to represent on the stage characters behaving badly or foolishly, so that the audience reforms to avoid being ridiculed in a similar way, the sentimental conception was to represent good people, suffering undeservedly and finally rewarded with happiness, or else—as we have seen with Cibber—erring human beings who have a fifth act repentance. The sentimentalists were distrustful of satiric comedy, and even of laughter. As Whitehead, one of the dramatists put it,

> That eager zeal to laugh the vice away
> May hurt some virtue's intermingling ray.

After Steele, the chief writers of sentimental comedy besides Whitehead were Cumberland and Kelly. All three possessed some dramatic talents—a power of depicting characters, sometimes original characters, and a sense of the stage—but they were all handicapped by a wrong theory of comedy and a tendency to write deplorably stilted dialogue. Cumberland is particularly guilty in this respect:

> Penruddock's myrmidons are in my house. Besides, there's worse than that—my son is come to England. Henry will be upon me, and to meet his gallant, injured presence would be worse than death.

*   *   *   *

> If fathers, whilst their sons are bleeding in their country's battles, will hurl the fatal dice, and stake their fortunes on the cast, alas for their posterity.

*   *   *   *

> What have I done, or the poor cat my peaceable companion, that thus the boisterous knuckles of the law should mar our meditations.

The absurd remoteness of such speeches from the language of real life was more damaging than the sentimentality.

Hugh Kelly, although he wrote sentimental comedies, was one of the first to satirise them. In *False Delicacy* (1768), he inserts a character, Mrs Harley, to satirise sentimentality, and we are meant to regard the false delicacy of the lovers as absurd. In *The School for Wives* (1774), Kelly again condemned sentimentality, but he still clung to the idea that comedy should be didactic:

Lady Rachel Instructive—why the modern Critics say that the only
    business of comedy is to make people laugh.
Belville That is degrading the dignity of letters exceedingly, as well as
    lessening the utility of the stage. A good comedy is a capital effort
    of genius, and should therefore be directed to the noblest purposes.
Miss Walsingham Very true: and unless we learn something while we
    chuckle, the carpenter who nails the pantomime together will be
    entitled to more applause than the best comic poet in the kingdom.

Throughout the eighteenth century there were attempts to stem
the tide of sentimentality. Before he found himself in the novel,
Fielding wrote a number of farcical comedies. Shaw lamented that
one who might have become a great dramatist was driven from the
theatre by the introduction of censorship, but his plays, though
refreshingly free of sentimentality, showed little sense of style.
More successful was *The Beggar's Opera* of John Gay—a ballad
opera which owed much of its success to its songs, but which
contains fresh and lively characters and first-rate dialogue. *Polly*,
the sequel, ran into trouble with the Lord Chamberlain, and was,
in any case, much less interesting.

When we come to the middle of the century the situation was
even worse. There were revivals of Congreve—bowdlerised—but the
new plays were all sentimental. Foote complained in 1768 that 'the
drama is directed by the genius of insipidity' and that the stage was
'a kind of circulating library for the vending of dialogue novels'.
In the same year the better side of the sentimental craze was shown
by the publication of *A Sentimental Journey*; but Sterne had wit,
humour and style, which the dramatists, generally speaking, had not.
Foote returned to the attack in *The Handsome Housemaid or Piety
in Pattens*, a puppet-show 'more refined than Punch and Judy', in
which 'not a single expression shall escape that can wound the nicest
ear or produce a blush on the most transparent skin'.

Another critic of the prevailing mode was Oliver Goldsmith. An
actor in *The Vicar of Wakefield*, apparently speaking for the author,
remarks that, 'the works of Congreve and Farquhar have too much
wit in them for the present taste'; and when Goldsmith, in his last
years, began writing for the stage, he tried to break away from the
current vogue. His two plays and three plays of Sheridan, all written
between 1772 and 1779, represent an attempt to return to the comic
tradition of the seventeenth century.

Goldsmith tells us in the preface to *The Good-Natured Man* that
he 'was strongly prepossessed in favour of the poets of the last age,
and strove to imitate them'; and he says that before the advent of

genteel comedy, 'little more was desired by an audience, than nature and humour'. The bailiffs scene had been severely cut in performance and Goldsmith hopes that, 'too much refinement will not banish humour and character from ours, as it has already done from the French theatre'. In the epistle dedicatory to *She Stoops to Conquer*, addressed to Dr Johnson, Goldsmith admitted that it was 'very dangerous' to undertake a comedy which was not merely senti-mental.

Sheridan expresses a similar uneasiness. In the second prologue of *The Rivals*, spoken on the tenth night, Sheridan points to the figure of comedy:

> Look on this form—where humour, quaint and sly,
> Dimples the cheek, and points the beaming eye;
> Where gay Invention seems to boast its wiles
> In amorous hint, and half-triumphant smiles;
> While her light mask o'er covers Satire's strokes,
> All hides the conscious blush her wit provokes.
> —Look on her well—does she seem formed to teach?
> Should you *expect* to hear this lady—preach?
> Is grey experience suited to her youth?
> Do solemn sentiments become that mouth?
> Bid her be grave, those lips should rebel prove
> To every theme that slanders mirth or love.
>
> Yet thus adorned with every graceful art
> To charm the fancy and yet reach the heart—
> Must we displace her? And instead advance
> The goddess of the woeful countenance—
> The sentimental Muse!

In fact, there is a residue of sentimentality in both Goldsmith and Sheridan. Honeywood, the hero of *The Good-Natured Man*, might have appeared in any sentimental comedy; and Goldsmith, though critical, is not satirical or humorous at the character's expense. Faulkland in *The Rivals*, whatever Sheridan's intentions, was not regarded as laughable by the original audiences; and, despite the satire of the moralising Joseph Surface in *The School for Scandal*, there is more than a trace of sentimentality in the presentation of his brother. But it would be wrong to exaggerate the extent to which the two dramatists were infected by the style they sought to avoid. For the only one of these plays which is seriously spoilt by the prevailing mode is *The Good-Natured Man*. When Sir William

Honeywood preaches to his nephew in the last scene of the play, the comic muse takes flight:

> Yes, sir, you are surprised to see me; and I own that a desire of correcting your follies led me hither. I saw, with indignation, the errors of a mind that only sought applause from others; that easiness of disposition, which, though inclined to the right, had not courage to condemn the wrong. I saw with regret those splendid errors, that still took name from some neighbouring duty. Your charity, that was but injustice; your benevolence, that was but weakness; and your friendship but credulity. I saw, with regret, great talents and extensive learning only employed to add sprightliness to error, and increase your perplexities. I saw your mind with a thousand natural charms; but the greatness of its beauty served only to heighten my pity for its prostitution.

Honeywood's foolishness should have been corrected in a less ponderous way—by the exposure of his false friend, Lofty, and by the raillery of Miss Richland—and nowhere in the play are we given evidence of 'great talents and extensive learning' or even of 'a thousand natural charms'. Mr L. J. Potts suggests that Goldsmith 'could not bring himself to see through this false good nature altogether'. Perhaps because he saw himself as the hero he 'wants us to feel that after all Honeywood really is rather nice, and that undermines the whole theme of the play, which is that he is a sham'.[1]

Goldsmith is most successful in the portrait of the pessimist Croaker. On his first appearance there is an effective use of repeated catch-phrases:

Croaker I hope this weather does not affect your spirits. To be sure, if this weather continues—I say nothing—But God send we be all better this day three months.
Honeyw. I heartily concur in the wish, though I own not in your apprehensions.
Croaker May be not! Indeed what signifies what weather we have in a country going to ruin like ours? Taxes rising and trade falling. Money flying out of the kingdom and Jesuits swarming into it. I know at this time no less than a hundred and twenty-seven Jesuits between Charing Cross and Temple Bar.
Honeyw. The Jesuits will scarce pervert you or me, I should hope.
Croaker May be not. Indeed what signifies whom they pervert in a country that has scarce any religion to lose? I'm only afraid for our wives and daughters.

[1] *Comedy* (1949), p. 115.

Honeyw. I have no apprehensions for the ladies, I assure you.
Croaker May be not. Indeed what signifies whether they be perverted or
    not. The women in my time were good for something. I have seen
    a lady dressed from top to toe in her own manufactures formerly.
    But nowadays, the devil a thing of their own manufactures about
    them, except their faces.

Even funnier is the scene in Act IV where Croaker misunderstands
the letter written to his son as a threat to blow up his house.
    The best of the remaining scenes is III.i where Honeywood tries
to pass off the Bailiffs as his friends, and has continually to interrupt
their remarks to Miss Richland lest their vulgarity should give them
away. The reactions of the critics to this scene—even though it was
cut in performance—led Goldsmith to retaliate in the tavern scene
in *She Stoops to Conquer*, where four of Tony Lumpkins's cronies
have the following conversation:

First Fellow The Squire has got spunk in him.
Second Fellow I loves to hear him sing, bekeays he never gives us
    nothing that's *low*.
Third Fellow O damn anything that's *low*, I cannot bear it.
Fourth Fellow The genteel thing is the genteel thing at any time. If so
    be that a gentleman bees in a concatenation accordingly.

She Stoops to Conquer is in every way an improvement on the
previous play. The trick by which Marlow takes Hardcastle's house
for an inn—however unlikely it might seem—was based on a true
incident, and it seems quite plausible in performance. Kate's
stratagem, of stooping to conquer, is also acceptable in the theatre,
given Marlow's split personality. Hastings and Miss Neville are
conventional lovers of no particular interest; but the remaining
characters—Hardcastle, his wife and Tony—are lively and convincing. Some scenes in the play are extremely funny—the rudeness
of Marlow and Hastings to the man they think is their landlord,
the first interview between Marlow and Kate—but what makes it
one of the most popular English comedies is neither its wit nor its
humour but the apparent affection Goldsmith has for his characters
—an affection which is shared by the audience. There are, however,
two faults in the play. The gentility of the age prevented Goldsmith
from persuading us that Marlow's behaviour was ever really
licentious; and his love speeches in the last scene of the play ring
false:

> By all that's good, I can have no happiness but what's in your power
> to grant me. Nor shall I ever feel repentance, but in not having seen
> your merits before. I will stay, even contrary to your wishes; and
> though you should persist to shun me, I will make my respectful
> assiduities atone for the levity of my past conduct.

Such a speech would have passed muster in a novel or an essay; and
it should be remembered that Goldsmith, although 'he touched
nothing he did not adorn', came to the theatre at the end of his
career. He was very successful in writing dialogue for low and
humorous characters; but in attempting to write in a loftier style
he became extremely stilted. He claimed that his models were the
dramatists of the previous century; but he was closer in spirit to
Farquhar than to Wycherley or Congreve.

Sheridan, too, looked to the Restoration dramatists as his models,
as can be seen from his revivals of *Love for Love* and *The Old
Bachelor* and his rewriting of *The Relapse* as *A Trip to Scarborough*.
His two masterpieces are, in fact, much closer in spirit to the Comedy
of Manners than either of Goldsmith's had been. *The Rivals* was
performed in 1775, less than two years after *She Stoops to Conquer*,
and it was badly received, partly because of indifferent acting and
partly because of Sheridan's inexperience as a playwright. The
comedy was criticised for its excessive length and, we are told, for
its 'weak puns and coarse innuendoes'. Sheridan expurgated all
these; he transformed the character of Sir Lucius O'Trigger and he
shortened the play considerably. As a result, when the revised
version was performed eleven days after the original, it was a
great success.

There are several rivals in the play: Captain Absolute, Sir Lucius
and Acres are all suitors for the hand of Lydia, not to mention
'Ensign Beverley'. The central situation, which is caused by the
romantic notions of Lydia, is admirably managed; and there is a
pleasant irony in the fact that Absolute seems less likely to succeed
in his suit with his father's approval than without it. The characterisation, though bordering on the farcical, provides actors with a
number of good parts, including such minor ones as Fag and Lucy.
The play deserves its popularity in the theatre.

But gay and amusing as it is, it comes a long way short of the best
comedies of manners. Much of the dialogue lacks the punch and
polish of first-rate comedy, and some of the characters are less
interesting than they once seemed—Sir Lucius and Acres, for
example. We may suspect, too, that Sheridan's audience took the

character of Faulkland more seriously than the dramatist intended. It was surely meant as a satirical portrait of a particular kind of neurotic, not as the sympathetic study of an exquisitely sensitive lover. Oddly enough, at one revival between the two wars, when the part was played by Claude Rains, several critics remarked that it was the most interesting character in the play.

These critics were, perhaps, carried away by a brilliant piece of acting in a rôle which few actors would choose. The favourite rôle is, of course, that of Mrs Malaprop, in which it is difficult to fail. Her 'derangement of epitaphs' is extremely funny:

> ... to illiterate him, I say, quite from your memory.

> ... I would by no means wish a daughter of mine to be a progeny of learning ...

> ... You forfeit my malevolence for ever.

> ... She's as headstrong as an allegory on the banks of Nile.

Sheridan is said to have derived the idea of malapropism for a character in *A Journey to Bath*, written by his mother. He may also have remembered some of Shakespeare's characters such as Dogberry or Mistress Quickly. The difference between these and Mrs Malaprop is significant. Dogberry is given comparatively few blunders and they are all quite plausible for a semi-literate constable in the sixteenth century, as, for example, *suspect* for *respect*, *opinioned* for *pinioned, aspicious* for *suspicious*. Mrs Malaprop, on the other hand, is given some sixty of such blunders, including ten in a single speech. Although theatrical characters are necessarily larger than life, we never entirely believe in Mrs Malaprop. This is partly because her social position makes her ignorance improbable, but also because someone with such a large vocabulary is unlikely to misapply so many words. Anyone who knew the word 'allegory' would not confuse it with an alligator. Sheridan is so anxious to get laughs that he has sacrificed the reality of his character.

The School for Scandal, described by Horace Walpole as 'a marvellous resurrection of the stage', was an almost accidental masterpiece. It was a combination of *The Slanderers* (written possibly in 1772 when Sheridan was recovering from the wounds he had received in a duel) and *The Teazles*.[1] According to a well-

[1] Thomas Moore, *Memoirs of the Life of . . . Sheridan* (1825), pp. 210–235. Some passages in these plays are remarkably close to the revised versions in *The School for Scandal*. Here, for example, is the opening scene of *The Slanderers* (the speakers are Lady Sneerwell and Spather):

known story, the play was not completed until the day of the first performance. Yet the finished product shows no signs of haste or carelessness. It is, indeed, well-constructed, the three plots being ingeniously interwoven. Joseph is a member of the School, is favoured by Sir Peter as Maria's suitor, and is the would-be seducer of Lady Teazle. The School goes into action after the discovery of Lady Teazle in Joseph's apartments. Lady Sneerwell and Maria are both in love with Charles. Sir Peter is an old friend of Sir Oliver; and, of course, until her reformation, Lady Teazle is a member of the School.

In spite of his admiration for Congreve and Vanbrugh, Sheridan has moved a long way from Restoration comedy in spirit. The old man who is foolish enough to marry a young wife is not in serious danger of being cuckolded. We are told that Charles is a profligate, but all we are shown is a harmless party, at which there are no women present, and at which everyone is sober; and perhaps the forgiveness of the prodigal merely because he refuses to sell his uncle's portrait is a little too easy. But Sheridan had learnt from the initial failure of *The Rivals* that his audience must not be shocked and he went as far as he dared in his portrayal of Joseph, whose moral sentiments are represented not merely as a cover for his

---

Lady S. The paragraphs, you say, were all inserted.

Spat. They were, madam.

Lady S. Did you circulate the report of Lady Brittle's intrigue with Captain Boastall?

Spat. Madam, by this Lady Brittle is the talk of half the town; and in a week will be treated as a demirep.

Lady S. What have you done as to the innuendo of Miss Niceley's fondness for her own footman?

Spat. 'Tis in a fair train, ma'am. I told it to my hair-dresser,—he courts a milliner's girl in Pall Mall, whose mistress has a first cousin who is waiting-woman to Lady Clackit. I think in about fourteen hours it must reach Lady Clackit, and then you know the business is done.

In the revised version, Sheridan condensed these speeches, omitting Miss Nicely altogether, but adding a dozen lines on the abilities of Mrs Clackit. Sheridan also improved the phrasing in numerous passages.

Spatter's speech 'True, ma'am, there are valetudinarians in reputation as in constitutions; and both are cautious from their appreciation and consciousness of their weak side, and avoid the least breath of air' becomes Sir Benjamin's

'There are valetudinarians in reputation as well as constitution; who, being conscious of their weak part, avoid the least breath of air, and supply the want of stamina by care and circumspection.'

Although this is a considerable improvement it still lacks the polish combined with colloquial ease of Congreve's dialogue.

hypocrisy, but almost as a sign of it. This had the effect of under-cutting the lofty remarks of many heroes of sentimental comedy. Yet, as Lamb pointed out in recalling Palmer's performance, Joseph is much more interesting than his brother. In the very first scene, he gives vent to a moral sentiment about Charles:

> . . . for the man who does not share in the distresses of a brother, even though merited by his own misconduct, deserves—

Lady Sneerwell interrupts:

> O Lud! you are going to be moral, and forget that you are among friends.

Even after he has been exposed, the habit of moralising is too strong for him. He proposes to follow Lady Sneerwell,

> lest her revengeful spirit should prompt her to injure my brother, I had certainly better follow her directly. For the man who attempts to—
> [He exits with his sentiment unfinished.]

The play has a succession of theatrically effective scenes: the meeting of the School, two quarrels between Sir Peter and Lady Teazle, the auction of Charles's ancestors, the expertly contrived screen scene (though it owes something to a French original), Joseph's refusal to help his uncle in disguise, the scene in which Sir Peter is rumoured to be dangerously wounded, and the scene in which the two brothers unite to expel their uncle—all these are excellent theatre. Sheridan writes straightforward colloquial dialogue, not particularly polished, but for that very reason preferred by most audiences to that of Congreve.

Lady Teaz. Lud, Sir Peter! Would you have me be out of the fashion?
Sir Peter The fashion indeed! what had you to do with fashion before you married me?
Lady Teaz. For my part, I should think you would like to have your wife thought a woman of taste.
Sir Peter Ay—there again—taste! Zounds! madam, you had no taste when you married me.

Sheridan should have left it there, but he makes Lady Teazle add:

> That's very true, indeed, Sir Peter! and after having married you, I should never pretend to taste again, I allow.

The explanation of the joke for the slower members of the audience is liable to irritate those who have already seen the point.[1]

Sheridan's last comedy, *The Critic*, amusing as it is, belongs to a different genre. *The School for Scandal* was the last important comedy—the last important play—for more than a century.

There was a revival of drama in the last decade of the nineteenth century. Bernard Shaw, who referred more than once to the brilliance of Congreve's dialogue and perhaps learnt from it, dissuaded Granville-Barker from reviving *The Way of the World*. This was not primarily due to his puritanism. Although he himself wrote on the relation between the sexes (in *The Philanderer* and *Man and Superman*), on marriage (in *Candida* and *Getting Married*), and even on the manners of the upper classes (in *Heartbreak House*), his method is obviously quite different from that of the comic writers of the seventeenth century. Whereas Congreve and Wycherley satirised aberrations from their conception of sensible, civilised behaviour, Shaw's avowed aim, at least in his early plays, was not to correct the vices and faults of individuals, but to change society. His comic genius was harnessed to moral passion.

Oscar Wilde was much closer in spirit to the Restoration dramatists. His dialogue with its artificial glitter and superficial epigrams is greatly superior to that of Pinero or Henry Arthur Jones; but three of his plots are, unfortunately, as melodramatic as theirs, and the characters are stereotypes—the woman with a past, the statesman whose career is built on dishonour, and so on. Only in *The Importance of Being Earnest* did Wilde emerge as a significant dramatist. The play has sometimes been classed as a comedy of manners, and it certainly does comment indirectly on the manners of society; but the sublime absurdity of the dialogue, the fantastic plot, and the characterisation all mark it out as the greatest of English farces rather than a belated comedy of manners.

[1] The following exchange is more subtle:

Sir Peter Ah, madam, true wit is more nearly allied to good nature than your ladyship is aware of.
Lady Teaz. True, Sir Peter: I believe they are so near akin that they can never be united.

Sir Benjamin Backbite adds 'Or rather, suppose them man and wife, because one seldom sees them together'. Most of the audience laugh at Lady Teazle's remark, and the remainder laugh at Sir Benjamin's. But Lady Teazle was referring to the prohibitions in the Table of Consanguinity, not to her marriage.

The revivals of Restoration comedies, and the changed climate of opinion which made them possible, led to a number of attempts to emulate them. Somerset Maugham, for example, satirised the manners and morals of a section of society in *Our Betters*. Where it failed was in the total lack of distinction in the dialogue.

It appears that comedy of manners requires equality between the sexes together with social inequality. The gradual erosion of class, a manifest good in itself, makes it increasingly difficult to write the kind of comedy with which we have been concerned in this book.

BIBLIOGRAPHY

The following texts have been used:

CONGREVE

The Complete Plays of William Congreve, Ed. Herbert Davis (Chicago, 1967).
[Some accidentals have been taken from the 1710 edition.]
The Mourning Bride, etc. Ed. B. Dobrée (1928).

DRYDEN

Four Comedies, Ed. L. A. Beaurline and F. Bowers (Chicago, 1967).
Dramatic Works, Ed. M. Summers (1931–2).

ETHEREGE

The Works of Sir George Etherege, Ed. H. F. B. Brett-Smith (1927).

FARQUHAR

The Complete Works of George Farquhar, Ed. Charles Stonehill (1930).

OTWAY

Works of Thomas Otway, Ed. J. C. Ghosh (1932).

SHADWELL

The Works of Thomas Shadwell, Ed. M. Summers (1927).
Select Plays, Ed. G. Saintsbury (1903).
The Virtuoso, Ed. M. H. Nicolson, D. Rodes (1966).

SOUTHERNE

Plays of Thomas Southerne (1774).

VANBRUGH

The Complete Works of Sir John Vanbrugh, Ed. B. Dobrée and G. Webb (1927–8).

WYCHERLEY

The Complete Plays of William Wycherley, Ed. G. Weales (New York, 1967).

CRITICISM

Bateson, F. W., *Essays in Criticism*, VII (1957), pp. 56 ff.
Brown, J. R., and Harris, B., *Restoration Theatre* (1965).
Collier, Jeremy, *A Short View of the Immorality and Profaneness of the English Stage* (1698).
Dobrée, Bonamy, *Restoration Comedy* (1924).
Fujimura, Thomas H., *The Restoration Comedy of Wit* (Princeton, 1952).
Holland, N. N., *The First Modern Comedies* (Harvard, 1959).
Knights, L. C., *Explorations* (1947).
Krutch, J. W., *Comedy and Conscience after the Restoration* (New York, 1924).
Loftis, J., *Comedy and Society from Congreve to Fielding* (Stanford, 1959).
Lynch, Kathleen M., *The Social Mode of Restoration Comedy* (New York, 1926).
Meredith, George, *An Essay on Comedy* (1897).
Mueschke, P. and M., *A New View of Congreve's Way of the World* (Ann Arbor, 1958).
Nicoll, Allardyce, *A History of English Drama* (1952).
Palmer, John, *The Comedy of Manners* (1913).
Smith, J. H., *The Gay Couple in Restoration Comedy* (Cambridge, Mass., 1948).
Stoll, E. E., *Shakespeare Studies* (1942).
Underwood, Dale, *Etherege and Seventeenth Century Comedy* (New Haven, 1957).
Wain, John, *Preliminary Essays* (1957).
Walpole, Horace, *Works*, vol. II (1798).
Woolf, Virginia, *The Moment* (1947).
Zimbardo, Rose A., *Wycherley's Drama* (1965).

INDEX